And Yet They Come

Portuguese Immigration
from the Azores to the United States

And Yet They Come
Portuguese Immigration
from the Azores to the United States

Jerry R. Williams

1982
CENTER FOR MIGRATION STUDIES
NEW YORK

*The Center for Migration Studies is an educational,
non profit institute founded in New York in 1964
to encourage and facilitate the study of socio-demographic,
economic, political, historical, legislative and pastoral
aspects of human migration and refugee movements.
The opinions expressed in this work are those of the author.*

Library of Congress Catalog Number 82-71501
ISBN 0-913256-57-9 (Cloth) 0-913256-60-9 (Paper)
Printed in the United States of America

Includes bibliographical references and index.

1. Azoreans—United States—History.
2. Azores—Emigration and immigration—History
3. United States—Emigration and immigration—History

And Yet They Come: Portuguese Immigration
from the Azores to the United States

JVC6974 W54   1982   325.245990973   82-12794

DEDICATION

This book is dedicated to
John and Sally Avila,
two very special people.

Acknowledgements

Although it is impossible to acknowledge all those who helped to make this book possible, I am particularly indebted to Hal Nelson, a former colleague who originally suggested that a study of Portuguese immigrants was long overdue, to Chuck Nelson for his cartographic assistance and to my long-time colleague and friend Bruce Bechtol for his continuing encouragement and support. Every manuscript needs a good typist and I was fortunate enough to have the services of Muriel Siry. The most valuable contribution to this study — time to read, to think and to write was provided by an NEH Fellowship and I am especially grateful for the support I received from the National Endowment for the Humanities. And, of course, all of the informants in this country and in the Azores who so graciously answered my questions and provided information deserve special recognition since this is really their story.

Contents

List of Tables

List of Maps

Introduction

Over the past ten years, ethnicity has reemerged as a topic of considerable interest in the United States and it appears to be accompanied by an ethnic revitalization on the part of many third, fourth and fifth generation descendents of former ethnic minorities. Given this interest in ethnicity and the variety of works appearing in the field, a study of one of these previously neglected ethnic groups[1] seems not only appropriate but long overdue. From nine small islands in the Atlantic Ocean, the Azores, came a group of immigrants who made little recognized contributions to this country. Their story is unique, in the sense that the experience of every one of the millions of immigrants who came to America was unique. They all left behind their families and friends, a familiar way of life, a sense of belonging, and set out for a strange new land where the language was foreign and the customs unfamiliar. Although many ethnic groups shared these experiences, for the individuals involved it was a personal experience and those memories remained with them for the rest of their lives.

While most of the larger ethnic groups in the United States have been studied, some of them repeatedly, and their story appropriately recorded, the Azoreans have been the subject of only a few localized reports — most of which were either generalized and erroneous or ended up as an academic exercise to be shelved and forgotten in some university

[1] I am using George DeVos' definition of an ethnic group — "A self-perceived group of people who hold in common a set of traditions not shared by the others with whom they are in contact". In George DeVos, "Ethnic Pluralism: Conflict and Accommodation". In *Ethnic Identity: Cultural Continuities and Change.* Edited by George DeVos and Lola Romanucci-Ross. Palo Alto: Mayfield, 1975. P. 9.

library. The contemporary descendents of those early immigrants who seek to learn "their story" long after their grandparents, and occasionally even their parents have died, discover that it is a difficult task at best. Yet, there are a number of characteristics of the Azorean migration that merit further study and recognition: the migration experience itself, which encompassed three distinct stages, 1800—1870, 1870—1920, and 1957 to the present; the role of familial ties in influencing settlement location and occupation of the immigrants; the roles of the immigrants and their descendents in the new society; the retention of the religious celebration and its symbolic and pragmatic functions for the group; and the unusual distribution pattern of Azoreans within the United States.

No single discipline provides an adequate framework for such a study. Rather, the divergent information on the subject suggests the need for a multi-disciplinary approach centered on a particular theme. The social sciences provide the methodology; the subject matter furnishes a universal theme — the migration experience. Every migration is at once a beginning and an end for the individuals involved. It is a first step in the direction of a future existence which, in most cases, differs radically from the present. Certainly for the Azoreans, migration brought an abrupt end to a way of life that had changed little in the past century. The stability imparted from living in the same village where one's parents and their parents before them had lived was left behind in the search for an unknown replacement.

The migration of an individual or a group of individuals involves much more than just the physical relocation from one place to another. If one accepts the idea that "migration is generated by significant differences between one area and another", [2] then it is necessary to understand what conditions were like at the time of the migration in both the sending and receiving areas. Every migration has one or more general causes that serve to emphasize the difference between the homeland and the country of reception. They may be political, economic, social, religious, technological or some combination of these, but they are sufficiently strong to convince the emigrant that there is at least a chance that life is better elsewhere. Even so, each migrant sees the situation through his, or her, own particular perspective and develops individual reasons for leaving the native land.

The migration of people from a traditional homeland to a new location is one of the central themes in the history of mankind. From

[2] Kingsley, Davis, "The Migrations of Human Populations", *Scientific American*, 231:100. Sept. 1974.

some obscure and, as yet, not completely documented origin, human beings gradually spread over the face of the earth long before the arrival of the first sailing ships we associate with the discovery of the New World. Although our knowledge of these earlier migrations is often fragmentary, and in many instances non-existent, one irrefutable fact remains — when Ferdinand Magellan circumnavigated the globe for the first time in 1519–22, the entire world, with the exception of Antartica, was already inhabited by human beings. Migration then is neither a recent nor a unique phenomenon in human existence but, rather, a universal solution by which individuals and groups cope with problems that periodically become too great to withstand. To forsake a known environment in which the individual and group have evolved a successful survival strategy, however difficult it might be, for an unknown and frequently unfamiliar habitat is not a risk lightly undertaken. The motivation for such action, while varied, is of necessity severe; otherwise cultural inertia would prevail against relocation.

Although the existence of significant differences between one area and another are at the heart of all migrations, the overt stimuli for specific migrations differ from place to place and time to time. They can, however, be grouped into two rather broad and general categories: 1) those resulting from natural causes over which individuals have little control; and 2) those resulting from man-induced causes. The former include a series of natural disasters which result, in the final analysis, in a shortage of foodstuffs and the creation of a hostile environment. Among these are such things as substantial and prolonged variations in seasonal norms manifested through devastating droughts or severe flooding; cataclysmic events associated with volcanic or seismic activity; and biological or botanical manifestations which severely reduce either the local animal or plant population upon which the human population is dependent. The need to secure adequate foodstuffs in light of such natural disasters traditionally resulted in the decision to move elsewhere.

Man-induced causes for migration are legion and include all of the social, political and economic manipulations common to our species. The breakdown of social interaction between two societies, which results in open warfare, is infamous as a cause of migration. Some leave to avoid having to fight a war; others to escape the ravages of conflict; and still others are forceably relocated by the victors. Economic conditions, although not so dramatic as war, can be equally destructive and repressive. A land tenure system where ownership is vested in the hands of a few and the rewards of hard labor are meager and sometimes non-existent often makes far off lands seem more attractive. Degradation of the environment, either through wanton exploitation or in an attempt to provide for a growing population, has frequently resulted in the inability of a particular environment to sustain a given number of people; and, again the only viable solution is to reduce the numbers dependent upon the land by migration. Also, of course, note must be made of the individual who possesses that insatiable desire to know what is on the other side of yonder mountain range or across some body of water. While satisfying that individual desire does not make for migration on a large scale, the stories such pioneers tell when they return of the lands of "milk and honey", of a paradise waiting to be claimed, have certainly encouraged people to migrate in search of a better life. The lives of the inhabitants of the Azores Islands have been touched at one time or another, by a variety of natural and man-induced disasters and, like their counterparts the world over, many have responded by seeking relief in a new homeland.

Once emigration is perceived as the best solution to a particular set of events, the problems of implementation arise. First, and foremost, is the decision of which country seems to provide the best opportunities and is willing to accept the individuals. Both of these conditions underwent considerable fluctuation in the nineteenth and especially the twentieth centuries. In most cases the future emigrants have to make their decisions about where to go on the basis of very limited information: word of mouth from individuals who have previously been in another country; letters from members of the immediate or extended family who have already relocated; bits of information in the local newspaper; and, advertisements extolling the opportunities in a particular country, provided of course, by transportation companies eager to sell a passage. Arranging payment for that passage frequently involved a number of secondary decisions. Options that were open to early immigrants, such as working as a ship's hand to pay for the passage, were no longer a possibility when the numbers of immigrants increased ten-fold or, more typically, a hundred-fold. Instead, it was often necessary to borrow the passage money with the understanding that it would be repaid after a job was secured in the new country. No one will ever know how many homes and farmsteads were used as collateral so that a son, husband, or daughter might make that initial journey.

That journey, motivated by a specific set of causes and undertaken after many deliberations and much soul searching, was a personal and unique experience. Taken collectively, however, the effects of this migration were long range, widespread and far reaching. The departure of thousands of emigrants from their homeland provided at least a temporary relief from too many people trying to eke out a living on too little land. In some cases, entire villages were depopulated and what had once been the case of an over abundance of labor became instead a shortage. An extensive system of agriculture utilizing more land but less labor took the place of the intensive agriculture formerly required to support a dense population on a limited amount of land. No longer living in the village of their birth and able to provide direct support to their elderly parents, many immigrants instead sent money and material goods from their new homes as surrogates for themselves. When, as occasionally happened, former emigrants returned to retire in their native land, or more typically, to enjoy an extended visit with loved ones left behind, they brought with them a new perspective on their former homeland and experiences about new ways of doing things which they were eager to share.

The arrival of thousands of immigrants from the Azores Islands left an equally discernible imprint upon their new homeland. The subsequent uneven pattern of distribution frequently resulted in large concentrations of poorly educated, Portuguese speaking newcomers in what could only be described as ghettos. Although the living conditions gradually improved, the inhabitants of several of these early urban concentrations acquired a particular niche in the urban economy which has continued to attract and hold subsequent migrants until the present. In addition, a substantial number drew upon their experiences as intensive cultivators in their native land and were instrumental in introducing new agricultural practices to a farming country. Still others utilized their knowledge of the seas in developing a livelihood and making a contribution. A universal aspect of the Azorean immigrants, wherever located in the United States, is the strong bond with the Catholic Church and the introduction of the religious celebrations so characteristic of their homeland. The existence of a Portuguese Hall and a religious celebration continues to be the most obvious indicator of their presence in a community.

For the last one hundred and fifty years, then, these former residents of nine small Atlantic islands have been making their way to the United States and now, increasingly, to Canada. Their numbers fluctuate in response to conditions in both their old homeland and the new. They continue to come, however, and their coming has had a substantial impact on life in the Azores Islands and in the areas where they have settled in America. To appreciate the effects of this migration, it is necessary to start even before these first individuals made their long journey and carefully trace the chain of events from that time to the present.

Chapter I

The Whaler:
A Slow Boat to America

No one sat down with pen in hand and noted the date when the first individual left the Azores for "America"; or, if there was such an account, it did not survive. It is probably just as well since many of the early departees left clandestinely and preferred that their leaving not be noted. It is clear, though, that the first significant migration from the Azores to the United States, its territories and future constitutent parts occurred during the 1800—1870 period. The impetus for the initial departures was as much the "pull" from America, in the form of jobs on whaling ships that were plying their trade in Azorean waters, as it was the "push" from a very traditional society isolated on nine small islands with little in the way of opportunity to offer the young inhabitants. Although the California gold rush and other attractions occurred during this period, the New England whalers were the dominant influence in providing the initial jobs, transportation, and future areas of settlement in America.

In the last half of the 20th century "whaling" has become a dirty word in the United States — an unlawful and despicable occupation that many would like to see banned worldwide. Such, however, was not always the case in this country. A great deal can and should be said about the accomplishments of the whalers who, for some three hundred years, made significant contributions to the American colonies and subsequently, United States.

The occasional killing of whales that swam along the coastline was already a well established pratice among the indigenous population when the first European colonist arrived to settle in the New England colonies. The new arrivals were quick to follow the example of the natives and, in some cases, even copied their hunting techniques. Throughout the 17th century shore whaling was sporadically carried on along the seaboard of the New York and New England colonies. Shore whalers lived along the coast and towed the captured whales to shore for processing. Most of the observation for whales took place from an elevated shore lookout which commanded a good view of the sea. When a whale spout was sighted, the crews were alerted, the boats launched and the hunt began. Dead whales were towed ashore where their blubber was removed, cut into small pieces and rendered in a process called "trying out". In good weather some shore whalers sailed along the coast, in sight of land, in search of whales which they then brought to the try pots on shore.[1] The success of the various shore whaling companies was primarily dependent upon the number of whales that chanced to swim close enough to shore to be observed and then pursued.

Early in the 18th century ships were outfitted for short voyages to search for whales away from the shoreline. Two desirable characteristics of the sperm whale became apparent about this time making this species the preferred target of these whalers. Sperm whales have a large closed cavity in their head which contains a mixture of spermaceti, a waxy solid used in making ointments and candles, and oil — the finest oil from whales. In addition to being sought for the superior quality of their oil, the bodies of dead sperm whales float and are thus less likely to be lost after they are killed than are the carcasses of other species of whales. On these early cruises, which lasted up to six weeks, the blubber was removed from the whale and stored in barrels aboard ship until the vessel returned to shore where the trying-out took place. The size of whaling ships gradually increased but the continued necessity of returning to port to render the voluminous blubber into oil served as the ultimate constraint to sailing range and time at sea. This restriction eventually prompted a major technological innovation among the whalers — the construction of a special area where the try pots could be housed on board and the trying-out completed at sea. Ship records indicate that some vessels were equipped with try works as early as 1762.[2] With the last major constraint lifted, whaling vessels sailed widely over the Atlantic Ocean in pursuit of their quarry during the last third of the 18th century — from the North Atlantic in the summer to the South Atlantic in winter.

[1] Alexander Starbuck, *History of the American Whale Fishery From Its Earliest Inception to the Year 1876.* New York, 1964. Pp. 1—20.

[2] *Ibid.,* P. 44.

In 1775, on the eve of the American Revolution, 304 vessels with a total of 4,059 seamen were employed in whaling — and most of those were out of Massachusetts.[3] Massachusetts dominated the whaling industry among the colonies from the beginning with the early centers of Nantucket and Cape Cod gradually being supplanted by New Bedford in the late 1700s — to the extent that New Bedford became the center of whaling in America during the 19th century. The losses suffered by the whalers and whaling ports were substantial during the Revolutionary War, as they were later during the War of 1812 and the Civil War of the 1860s, but each time the industry rebounded after the cessation of hostilities.

In 1787 the first whalers sailed into the Pacific Ocean and returned with reports of unlimited whaling.[4] The fleet continued to expand to work the traditional whaling grounds in the Atlantic and to explore the seemingly endless possibilities in the Pacific. By the early part of the 19th century it became increasingly difficult to find enough crewmen to man the growing whaling fleet. Instead of receiving a set wage, the crew of the whaler participated in a form of profit sharing called the lay system; it minimized the ship's expenses and motivated the crew to spot and kill every whale possible. When a ship returned from a cruise, the whale products were sold at the going rate and the expenses incurred in outfitting the ship were deducted, as were the owners' share of the profits. The remainder was divided among the crew based on their relative importance to the whaling operation as indicated by the pay they agreed to when they signed on the voyage — the captain and officers of the crew received the largest shares and the common sailors the smallest. Any supplies that a crewman needed while at sea were provided from the ship's stores and charged against the individual's share. While the lay system proved to be quite lucrative for the owners of the ships and usually rewarding for the officers and primary crew members, the common sailor frequently had little to show at the conclusion of a lengthy voyage. The Revolutionary War had extracted a heavy toll on the whaling industry, but by the early 1800s shipping out on a whaler did not offer the same attraction that it had a half century earlier. Given the existence of the lay system, the rewards from whaling for a common sailor were not nearly so certain as the hardships of a lengthy voyage. Other opportunities on the expanding western frontier seemed more attractive to many young men. It

---

[2] Charles Scammon, *The Marine Mammals of the North-Western Coast of North America.* San Francisco, 1874. P. 209.

[4] *Ibid.*

soon became common practice to obtain Americans for the ships' principal officers and sign on the remainder of the crew wherever they could be found. One place where they were easily recruited was a small group of islands in the Atlantic known as the Azores or Western Islands. The waters in the vicinity of the islands were a feeding ground for sperm whales and the New Englanders had become well acquainted with the islands in their pursuit of these whales.

What began as a small number of Azoreans shipping as crewmen on the whalers in the 1820s rapidly increased as the whaling fleet continued to expand in the 1840s and '50s and living conditions in the islands deteriorated. In the novel, *Moby Dick* , which the author based on his experience as a crewman on whaling vessels in 1841 and 1842, Herman Melville indicated that less than half of the seamen employed in the American whale fishery were Americans; they constituted virtually all of the officers, but most of the crewmen were recruited elsewhere.

No small number of these whaling seamen belong to the Azores, where the outward bound Nantucket whalers frequently touch to augment their crews from the hardy peasants of those rocky shores.[5]

The life of a seaman on an American whaling vessel with its deprivations, lengthy voyages and frequently meager rewards was certainly no easier for the Azoreans than it had been for the American sailors. Yet, they signed on in increasing numbers and proved themselves so well that they were soon "sought after by the masters for their daring pursuit of the fish, as well as for their quiet behavior on board".[6] Such accounts reveal a great deal about the nature of the people who inhabited these islands, but they also indicate that conditions there must have been very austere for so many young men to abandon their homeland for a life on board an American whaler.

The Azores lie between 36° 55' and 39° 43' north latitude and 25° and 31° 30' west longitude and are the only island chain in the mid-Atlantic. Some 2,000 miles east of Massachusetts, 700 miles off the coast of Portugal and 750 miles from Africa, they were ideally situated as a stopping point for outward-bound whalers desiring to replenish their supplies of vegetables and other fresh provisions before heading for the southern

[5] Herman Melville, *Moby Dick or The Whale.* New York, 1950. P. 118.

[6] Walter Frederick Walker, *The Azores or Western Islands: A Political, Commercial and Geographical Account.* London, 1886. P. 279.

fishery. From Flores, the most westerly island, the archipelago extends along a northwest-southeast line some 375 miles to Santa Maria, the most southeasterly island. Collectively known as the Azores, the chain actually consists of three groups of islands: Santa Maria and Sao Miguel — the most easterly pair; Terceira, Graciosa, Sao Jorge, Pico and Faial — the central group; and Corvo and Flores — situated on the northwest periphery of the archipelago[7] (*See,* Map 1). A rugged, inhospitable shoreline greeted the New England whalers when they reached the Azores; in the nine islands only Horta, Faial and Ponta Delgada, Sao Miguel had a protected harbor. These two became regular ports of call for many of the Atlantic whalers, both as a source of fresh supplies and as a depot and transshipment point for whale oil and bones.

The Azoreans quickly learned that whaling was a hard life, but so was the struggle to survive in their homeland. At the conclusion of each voyage the whaling vessels returned to their home port, which was almost always in Massachusetts and frequently was the port of New Bedford. Once the catch was sold the crew was paid and released and the ship was outfitted for a new cruise. After a short stay in port, most sailors shipped out on another voyage. Far from home, the islanders had the choice of staying in an unfamiliar land or returning to the now familiar sea; most of these sailors continued as whalemen in the 1820s and '30s. A few returned to the islands with tales to tell about the life of a whaler and this new country with unlimited land and great opportunities. Such stories must have made the bleak existence in the Azores seem even bleaker and many young men, after asking themselves, "Why stay?" and unable to think of a satisfactory answer, decided to try whaling. The initial voyage convinced many novice sailors that there must be a better way of earning a living than endlessly pursuing whales around the globe; for them the first voyage was also the last. Most often they ended up in Massachusetts, less frequently in California and occasionally in Hawaii. But, the Azores had a surplus population, and there were always new recruits ready to take the places of their countrymen. With the expansion of the whaling fleet in the 1840s and '50s, there was seldom any difficulty in finding a ship that needed crewmen. In the 1840s, the American whaleship was seen not only as an alternative itself to a difficult life in the islands, but increasingly as a way to get to America. Granted, it was a slow voyage, two and three year cruises were not uncommon then, and it was a hard life. With any luck, though, an individual could end up in

[7] James H. Guill, *A History of the Azores Islands.* Menlo Park, 1972. P. 26.

MAP 1

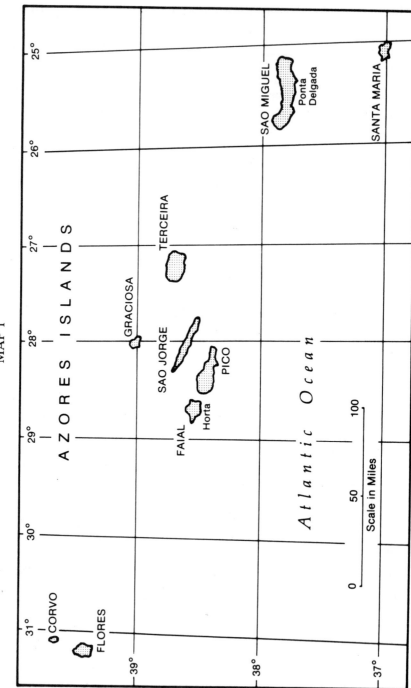

America without having spent any money for his passage, and, even have enough money from his share of the voyage to enable him to get settled. [8]

Two events occurred in the early 1850s which further stimulated the exodus of young men from the islands to the whale boats. The first of these was a disastrous decline in agricultural productivity in the Azores. A potato rot struck at the heart of the main subsistence crop while a new vineyard disease severely curtailed wine production. This new threat to agricultural self-sufficiency only served to enhance the attractiveness of whaling. The second event actually occurred in 1849 in a distant land called California, but its impact was felt in the Azores for the next twenty years. Whaleships brought the news of the gold strike in California to the islands and then, unwittingly, provided the transportation to get there — albeit indirectly. In 1850 the Nantucket and New Bedford fleets were whaling in the Arctic waters of the Pacific Ocean — an eighteen thousand mile voyage down the east coast of South America around Cape Horn and up the west coast to the bowhead whaling grounds on the north shores of Alaska.[9] San Francisco was a regular port of call for these ships; the port provided a final opportunity to replenish supplies before completing the journey to the Alaskan whaling grounds. Stories of gold waiting to be picked up and fortunes easily made were tempting to these sailors; many took advantage of the opportunity by deserting their ship and striking out for the gold fields. Desertion was a problem with which the captains of whaling ships always had to contend. After the discovery of gold, however, desertions reached epidemic proportions. One historian noted that "after the discovery of the gold mines in California, desertions from the ships were numerous and often causeless, generally in such numbers as to seriously cripple the efficiency of the ships".[10] Azoreans, and many others, availed themselves of this cheap and illegal passage to California. By the end of the 1850s whaling ships were forced to pay advance wages as an inducement to recruit seamen for their crews. Even so, the fleet was plagued with bounty-jumpers who took the advance pay and deserted at the first opportunity.[11] "There were times, when the California fever was at its highest, that the desertions did not stop with the men, but officers and even captains seem to vie with the crew" in leaving

[8] Josef Berger, *In Great Waters: The Story of the Portuguese Fishermen.* New York, 1941. Pp. 45–46.

[9] J.T. Jenkins, *A History of the Whale Fisheries.* New York, 1971. P. 234.

[10] Starbuck, *History of the American Whale Fishery.* P. 112.

[11] *Ibid.*

their ships.[12] San Francisco Bay and the Sacramento River were the last port that many whaling ships ever made and, without a doubt, the discovery of gold in California contributed to the eventual demise of whaling in the United States. Many whaling vessels began avoiding San Francisco, in an attempt to hold on to their crews, and the Hawaiian Islands became a center for refitting and supplying the Pacific whaling fleet. Desertions, however, remained a serious problem throughout the 1850s and '60s. In spite of the desertions in California, the Azoreans acquired a reputation as hard working, dependable whalers, and the practice of sailing from New England to the Azores, with a skeleton crew which would be filled out with islanders, became commonplace in the 1850s.

The aura of the gold fields and the general attraction of California continued to draw Azoreans from their island home to America, but now the majority of the newcomers ended up on the west coast instead of the east. Between 1860 and 1870, the number of Portuguese in California doubled and reached a new high of 3,435 — forty percent of the Portuguese population in the United States. By 1870, the pattern had been well established for the substantial out-migration from the Azores Islands to the United States that occurred between 1870 and 1921: Azoreans were well settled in the coastal areas of Massachusetts, primarily around whaling centers such as New Bedford, and Rhode Island; in the twenty years between 1850 and 1870, California became the leading center of Portuguese settlement and, if gold mining had not proved to be lucrative, farming had; a network of communications and extended familial ties was thereby established between friends and relatives in America and the Azores which encouraged migration, provided temporary housing for new immigrants, and helped them locate jobs. Although relatively small in number, the importance of these early immigrants in establishing the patterns of settlement and social networks[13] which subsequent immigrants relied on so heavily cannot be over-emphasized.

The men from the Azores Islands continued to fill the ranks of the whaling fleet in the 1860s and '70s and to a lesser extent, due

---

[12] *Ibid.*

[13] An individual's personal network consists of the chains of persons with whom that individual is in actual contact, and their interconnections. A social network is the composite of individual communication networks within a given society. For a discussion of social networks *see* Jeremy Boissevain, *Friends of Friends: Networks, Manipulators and Coalitions.* Oxford, 1974. Pp. 24—78.

to the decline of the industry, throughout the remainder of the century. Azoreans also manned shore whaling stations in various places around the world, prompting one authority on whaling to write that, "Afloat and ashore the islanders were ubiquitous in the nineteenth-century whaling scene".[14] The practice of signing on a whaler to get free passage to America became an established tradition in the islands and was employed by thousands of young men. This "before the mast" migration, so named because the common sailor's quarters were forward on a whaling ship, in front of the mast, while the officers' quarters were aft, brought the first Portuguese immigrants to New England, California and Hawaii.

[14] Robert Clarke, "Open Boat Whaling in the Azores", *Discovery Reports,* 26. P. 352.

Chapter II

The New England Habitat

Given living and working conditions on American whaleships in the 19th century, getting to America via a whaler was no mean accomplishment. Once the ship docked and the crew was paid and discharged, however, there was no shortage of opportunities for the former whaler now turned immigrant. As the activity in New Bedford demonstrated, there was much more to whaling than just chasing and killing whales. "With its oil refineries (whale oil), cooper's shops, tool-works, and the hundred-and-one industries subsidiary to whaling, New Bedford became a hive of industry...".[15] With a population of about 20,000 in 1857, the year that whaling reached its apogee, in terms of capital and tonnage involved, New Bedford alone had a fleet of 329 ships, worth more than twelve million dollars and manned by more than ten thousand seamen. [16] To maintain, outfit and supply these ships with the goods necessary to sustain them on a three or four year voyage was a monumental task requiring organizational expertise and strong backs. The New England businessmen provided the former and many a reformed whaler furnished the latter. In addition to preparing the ships for departure, the whale oil and bone brought in by these vessels had to be processed into oil for lubrication or burning, medical ointments, candles, corset staves and dozens of other by-products. Although New Bedford was the principal whaling port in America, the same scene, on a reduced scale, was repeated in numerous other ports along the coast of Massachusetts.

[15] Samuel Eliot Morison, *The Maritime History of Massachusetts 1783—1860.* P. 316.

[16] Zeph W. Pease and George A. Hough, *New Bedford, Massachusetts: Its History, Institutions and Attractions.* New Bedford, 1889. P.31.

For the islanders enamored with the sea, but disenchanted with whaling, numerous opportunities for either short or long voyages presented themselves. The cod and mackerel fisheries of Massachusetts were an important part of the 19th century economy and were a natural choice for confirmed fishermen no longer eager to undergo the trials of whaling. In 1855 the various ports in Massachusetts sent 1,138 ships, manned by 10,419 hands, to the cod and mackerel fisheries. Ten years later the number of men employed reached 11,358 and Cape Cod alone sent 314 ships and 3,832 men after these fish.[17] By the 1860s when the whaling industry began its gradual but steady decline, a number of Portuguese whalers had worked their way from "before the mast" to positions of authority on the aft decks. For these captains and officers, who had known no other life but the sea, the cod and mackerel fisheries were a logical alternative to whaling — and many took advantage of the opportunity.[18]

In addition to being the center of whaling and cod fishing, Massachusetts was also in the forefront of both the coastal trade that took place between the individual states and the deep water trade to and from various world ports. The port of Boston was second only to New York in commercial traffic and merchant ships vied with whalers and fishing vessels for crewmen. Low pay and less than ideal working conditions made it difficult to recruit seamen and "few Americans could be found in the forecastles of merchantmen on deep waters".[19] For the Azorean who had become a confirmed sailor, America provided no dearth of opportunities on the sea.

The first taste of the sea, provided by the whalers, was more than enough for most of them and they turned to other occupations; raised in a traditional agrarian society, they were, first and foremost, farmers. The hinterland of New Bedford and nearby Providence, Rhode Island, had been occupied and farmed for almost 250 years so that idle land suitable for farming was virtually non-existent. Farm laborers, not unlike sailors, typically worked long hours for low wages and dissatisfaction with life as a farmhand was almost as prevalent as it was among whalers. There were always jobs to be had as hired hands on local farms, though, and a number of these young men from the Azores applied themselves to a traditional occupation that

---

[17] Morison, *The Maritime History of Massachusetts.* P. 375.

[18] Berger, *In Great Waters.* Pp. 53—61.

[19] Morison, *The Maritime History of Massachusetts.* P. 352.

they knew intimately from first-hand experience. Skilled at squeezing a living from a small piece of land, some went on to become farmers themselves — first renting or working a small piece of land on a share basis and then gradually acquiring enough capital to purchase their own farm.

Massachusetts was more than ports and farmland in the 19th century; it was also at the heart of the industrial revolution sweeping across the United States. The rivers and streams that dropped down out of the Massachusetts hinterland to the sea were impossible to navigate, but an excellent source of cheap power. These streams were harnessed, up and down the coast, to drive the machinery of industrial development. Cotton mills, where raw fibers were converted into finished materials, sprang into life all along this fall line in the early 1800s. The first cotton mill in Fall River, a port town fourteen miles west of New Bedford and eighteen miles southeast of Providence, began production in 1813; sixty years later the textile mills in Fall River were employing in excess of ten thousand workers.[20] New Bedford, although preoccupied with whaling, eventually perceived the advantages of a more assured industrial base and its first cotton mill went into operation in 1849; others followed, and by 1870 the city's four mills provided jobs for about two thousand industrial workers.[21]

In addition to cheap power to drive the machinery, industry in the mid-1800s required abundant supplies of unskilled labor. Immigrants provided the poorly paid, unskilled labor force that industrialized the United States and the Portuguese made their contributions. The Azores were much further removed from the industrial world than the mere nautical distances to the mainland of Europe or America would indicate. A subsistence, agrarian economy has little demand for either skilled or educated workers and the vast majority of the islanders were neither skilled nor educated. Textile mills are ideally suited for just such a work force; labor intensive by nature, few jobs required more than minimal training. To be a bobbin boy, doffer, carder, comber, sweeper, spooler or any one of the other numerous semi-skilled occupations involved in manufacturing material from fiber did not require understanding the principles of hydraulic power or the operation of a mechanical loom; all that was necessary was to be able to stay awake, and perform a tedious, repetitive task in an unpleasant environment for ten

---

[20] Leading Manufacturers and Merchants of Eastern Massachusetts: Historical and Descriptive Review of the Industrial Enterprises of Bristol, Plymouth, Norfolk and Middlesex Counties. New York, 188?. Pp. 30—36.

[21] Pease, New Bedford, Massachusetts. Pp. 149—153.

or twelve hours a day. The mills of New Bedford, Fall River and Providence seemed to have an insatiable demand for laborers and many Azoreans joined the ranks of the "industrial workers". Few in number in the 1850s, Azorean mill workers gradually increased in the '60s and '70s and paved the way for their countrymen who poured into this area in subsequent decades.

When the young immigrant from the Azores stepped ashore in New England in the early 1870s, his compatriots had already established themselves in a number of occupational niches and were, in effect, holding the doors open to their fellow countrymen. The social network which was all pervasive in the islands also extended to family members living in the United States and it effectively spared most new immigrants from undue anxiety about their new life. For the most part, they joined members of their extended family or friends, either on a temporary or a more permanent basis, and relied heavily upon them for advice in finding jobs and arranging living accommodations. The existence of this effective social network between family members in the islands and the United States played a major role in determining where the post-1870 immigrants settled and strongly influenced the occupational opportunities available to them. The Portuguese immigrants living in the United States in 1870 were highly concentrated, not just in a few states, but in and around a relatively small number of communities within those few states. Former whaling centers, such as New Bedford, Providence and New Haven, were the primary centers in Massachusetts, Rhode Island and Connecticut, while in California, Oakland and the San Francisco Bay area, the entrance to the gold fields had become the focal point.

In 1870, when the first stage in the migration of the Azores Islanders to America was being transformed into the beginning of stage two, the official census of the United States reported 8,971 Portuguese living in this country and its territories.[22] In that particular census, Portuguese included those individuals from the Atlantic Islands (the Azores, Madeira and Cape Verde Islands) and mainland Portugal. The census also distinguished between white and colored; of the 8,971 Portuguese 257 were classified as colored and were, no doubt, former whalers from the Cape Verde Islands — a small group of black-inhabited islands off the west coast of Africa that belong to Portugal. Another 109 of the total were living in territories belonging to the United States. Although one or more Portuguese were reported in thirty-six of the thirty-seven states in that census, most were concentrated in

[22] *Ninth Census of the United States, 1870.* Vol. 1.

a few locations on the east and west coast.[23] With 2,555 Portuguese, Massachusetts accounted for thirty percent of the U.S. total and one out of every five of these immigrants (513) was living in Boston. The Portuguese population of New Bedford was sufficiently large in 1867 to justify sending a permanent Catholic priest to care for them; two years later their number was estimated at eight hundred.[24] Lesser numbers were found in New York (334 — 4%), Connecticut (221 — 2.6%) and Rhode Island (189 — 2.2%), but these four states collectively contained thirty-six percent of the Portuguese population in 1870. The other major concentration was in California, where 3,435 Portuguese, forty percent of the U.S. total, were living at that time.[25]

Throughout the second stage of migration, the new immigrants, for the most part, chose as their destination those places where friends and relatives had already established themselves and were encouraging others to join them. Massachusetts was the ideal destination for many of the new immigrants: a sizeable Portuguese population already resided in the state; it was one of the easiest locations to get to from the Azores, which meant lower transportation costs; and employment opportunities were readily available. By 1900 Massachusetts had surpassed California and could lay claim to having the largest Portuguese population in the country. Limited by their general lack of education and their unfamiliarity with industrial machinery, the early Portuguese immigrants in Massachusetts were primarily concentrated in a relatively small number of occupational categories: sea-related — whaling, fishing and sailing; agricultural oriented — farm laborers and small scale farmers; or, unskilled industrial workers in labor intensive mills. Whaling declined steadily after the 1870s, but it continued to be a viable occupation for a limited number of seamen; never again, however, did it provide jobs in quantities comparable to the 1840s and 1850s. Seafaring jobs were much more likely in Provincetown and Gloucester where the fleets departed for the Grand Banks of Newfoundland in search of codfish and halibut. The greatest demand, however, was for men and women to work in the flourishing textile mills of Fall River, New Bedford, Taunton, Lowell, and

---

[23] One-tenth of the total Portuguese population of the United States in 1870 was accounted for by a group of 856 Madeira Islanders who had been driven out of their homeland because they had converted to the Presbyterian religion; the Presbyterian Church in the United States subsequently went to their aid and helped resettle them in Illinois. *See:* Sandra Wolforth *The Portuguese in America.* San Francisco, 1978. P. 10.

[24] Donald R. Taft, *Two Portuguese Communities in New England.* New York, 1967. P. 97.

[25] *Ninth Census of the United States, 1870.* Vol. 1.

Lawrence, Massachusetts, and after 1890 the majority of the newcomers ended up in one of these mill towns.

Although the Census of 1870 did not record how many second generation Portuguese were living in Massachusetts, the foreign born Portuguese population of the state was 2,555; many of them had been residents of New Bedford for twenty years or more and undoubtedly had a number of children. Most of the Portuguese lived either in Bristol County, where both New Bedford and Fall River are located, or on nearby Cape Cod — especially in the fishing community of Provincetown at the tip of the Cape. They could also be found, to a lesser degree, scattered in the many fishing communities along the Massachusetts coast; the major fishing ports, such as Gloucester, in the extreme northern part of the state, also had a fairly substantial Portuguese population. The sea-oriented industries of New England have always expanded and contracted in response to current economic conditions and such was certainly the case at the end of the 19th century. The increased scarcity of whales and competition from petroleum products after 1870 resulted in a substantial decline in that particular industry, but the impact was partially offset by an expansion in banks fishing. The Grand Bankers, ships fitted out for a five or six month fishing voyage in search of codfish and halibut, derived their name from the Grand Banks of Newfoundland where they did most of their fishing. Provincetown was the center of Grand Banks fishing in Massachusetts and, as such, it attracted many of the early Portuguese immigrants who came over between 1870 and 1890. In the Provincetown fleet, "most of the skippers were men from the Azores, and their countrymen kept coming over to fill up the crew lists".[26]

The Grand Banks fleet reached its maximum expansion about 1885, but it continued to be an important industry until after the turn of the century. After 1880 it was gradually superseded by a growing all-season fishing fleet that provides fresh fish for the urban centers of Boston and New York. Provincetown also took the lead in developing the fresh-fish fleet and Portuguese fisherman owned and operated many of the boats. The regular supply of fresh fish and connecting overnight rail service between Boston and New York gradually established the port of Boston as the center of the Atlantic fishery.[27] Portuguese continued to occupy an important role in the fishing fleets of Massachusetts in the 20th century, but

[26] Berger, *In Great Waters,* P. 58.

[27] *Ibid.* P. 79.

the relative importance of fishing as an industry had long since been overshadowed by the industrial developments taking place within the state. By the second decade of the 20th century, it was noted that,

> The Portuguese are still prominent in fishing and other sea-faring occupations but their total number in these pursuits, though considerable, is not great when compared with those in the textile mills.[28]

After 1890, the flow of Portuguese immigrants increased dramatically and their numbers alone forced them to seek employment in industries with more intensive labor demands. They still continued to come to the areas where the first Portuguese had settled, but new modes of transportation were required. Instead of taking two or three years to work their way over on whaleships, many of the immigrants took advantage of the packet lines which were providing regular service between New Bedford and the Azores. The volume of traffic was sufficient for the barkentine, *Moses B. Tower,* for example, to make four regular trips a year between New Bedford and the Islands in 1889.[29] In place of the traditional jobs in whaling and fishing fleets, most of the new immigrants found employment in the cotton mills or related industries.

New Bedford succeeded in transforming itself from the whaling center of the United States in the 1850s to a major textile manufacturing center with 2,600 workers employed in the cotton mills in 1889.[30] Even though wages for unskilled labor in the mills were low, jobs were easy to get and the pay was superior to many other unskilled jobs in the area. One sixteen-year-old boy, who had just arrived from the island of Pico, got a job working for a Portuguese farmer on the outskirts of New Bedford for "five dollars a month, plus room and board".[31] It took him just two weeks to realize that there were more rewarding employment possibilities available. Through a friend he was able to get a job in one of New Bedford's cotton mills at $3.50 a week. Out of that $3.50 he had to pay room and board, but it only came to $2.50 a week and included his laundry. Farming could not compete with industry and, as the boy later recalled, "I went to work, sweeping floors in a cotton mill. In about three months, I was promoted to

---

[28] Taft, *Two Portuguese Communities in New England.* P. 134.

[29] Pease, *New Bedford, Massachusetts.* P. 65.

[30] *Ibid.* P. 153.

[31] Lawrence Oliver, *Never Backward: The Autobiography of Lawrence Oliver, a Portuguese American.* San Diego, 1972. P. 15.

being a cleaner...".[32] By 1910 New Bedford had become the center of the manufacturing of fine cotton goods in the United States.[33]

It was in the nearby town of Fall River, the largest textile center in the nation from 1880 until about 1920, that the Portuguese immigrants in New England attained their greatest concentration. The increasing demand for textiles was met by building more and larger mills and employing immigrant men, women, and children to provide the labor. Fall River grew from 74,398 in 1890 to over 100,000 in 1900 when 26,371 individuals, one-quarter of the total population, were employed as textile workers.[34] The Portuguese population of Fall River, which numbered only 104 in 1880, steadily grew to over 500 in 1900 and then the number suddenly exploded. In 1905 the city had 5,000 Portuguese immigrants, five years later there were more than 10,000.[35] After 1910 Fall River's growth rate started to slow down, but the Portuguese kept coming; in 1920, 22,431 of the city's 120,458 inhabitants were Portuguese.[36] They were the largest single foreign-born immigrant group in 1920 when they constituted 18.6 percent of the city's total population.[37] In addition to the Portuguese, however, there were also substantial numbers of Polish, Italian, and Russian immigrants in the city. Many members of the ethnic groups that had traditionally provided the labor for the textile mills during the last part of the 19th century, the English, Irish, and French Canadians, left the Fall River mills during a bitter twenty-six week strike in 1904 and did not return.[38]

> The Portuguese, and to a lesser extent the Poles, became the major source of unskilled operatives after 1900 — as the French Canadians had been in the 1870s. About half of Fall River's entire Portuguese and Polish population was working in the mills by 1910.[39]

[32] *Ibid.* P. 17.

[33] Seymour Louis Wolfbein, *The Decline of a Cotton Textile City: A Study of New Bedford.* New York, 1944. P.10.

[34] Philip T. Silva, Jr., "The Position of 'New' Immigrants in the Fall River Textile Industry", *International Migration Review,* 10(2):221. Summer 1976.

[35] *Ibid.* Pp. 224—225.

[36] Taft, *Two Portuguese Communities in New England.* P. 199.

[37] *Ibid.* P. 201.

[38] Silva, "The Position of 'New' Immigrants in the Fall River Textile Industry". Pp. 222—223.

[39] *Ibid.* P. 225.

The demand for textiles and the abundant supply of cheap immigrant labor that kept the mills running created a boom economy in Fall River and similar mill towns in Massachusetts and Rhode Island. The benefits, however, did not diffuse to the members of society as a whole. The immigrant populations were massed at the bottom of the social and economic ladder and suffered grievously from low wages, poor working conditions overcrowded housing, and inadequate health and social services. Unskilled and uneducated, the Portuguese filled the lower-paying occupational categories in the mills. Economic necessity motivated most of the able-bodied members of a family to seek employment in the mills where women and children, as well as men, became industrial workers. "If they marry, they must either live on a very low plane or expect their wives and children to continue to work outside the home...".[40] Working outside the home was not new to Portuguese women and children, it was a part of life in the sub-sistence-agarian economy of their homeland. Working conditions were quite different in the cotton mills than they had been in the fields, however, and the differences soon began to show themselves, albeit, in a subtle and devious fashion.

By 1910 the Portuguese in Fall River and New Bedford were attracting attention by their excessive infant mortality rates which were among the highest in the nation. In both communities the Portuguese suffered infant mortality rates in excess of 200 per 1,000 births — more than double the national average![41] The continued high infant mortality rates for Portuguese mothers prompted a number of studies which attempted to isolate the major factors responsible for the elevated number of infant deaths. Among the variables considered were: ethnicity, level of education, ability to speak English, living conditions, length of residence in the United States, whether or not the mother breast-fed her baby, and income level. A perceptive Fall River doctor concluded that:

> The foreign-born mother in Fall River, for example,
> is more likely to work in the mills during pregnancy,
> to have many children, and to live in crowded and
> unhygenic quarters. She, more than the native mother,
> reflects the injurious influences of an unfavorable
> industrial and economic climate.[42]

[40] Taft, *Two Portuguese Communities in New England.* P. 247.

[41] *Ibid.* P. 166.

[42] *Ibid.* P. 164.

The subsequent studies revealed that Portuguese mothers in Fall River were employed to a larger degree than mothers of any other nationality and that thirty-nine percent of the Portuguese mothers were employed outside their household during pregnancy — which was more than double the rate for other expectant mothers in the community.[43]

In the face of economic adversity, the forces which sustained the Portuguese immigrants in the mill towns of New England were the same forces which had sustained them in their homeland: their family, religion, and community. They came to the United States in search of economic opportunity, and if that meant that every able-bodied member of the family had to take a job in a factory, then they all took a job in a factory. Uneducated themselves, for the most part, Portuguese parents saw little need for their children to receive an education. While schools were a convenient place to send the young children, particularly if the mother had to work, for the older children it merely delayed their entry into a paying occupation which would assist the family. Most of the children of immigrant parents left school as soon as the law permitted and sought employment.[44]

The Portuguese population of Fall River in 1920, some 22,431 individuals, was a young, expanding population in need of housing and living space. Forty-five percent of the Portuguese community had been born in the United States and 30 percent were nine years old or younger. Children 14 years old and younger made up 41 percent of the population while only eleven percent of the total population was more than 45 years old.[45] The large number of poorly paid immigrants were hard-pressed to find adequate housing in Fall River and usually ended up with their families crowded into tenement houses.

> The sections of the city where most of the Portuguese live are unattractive. There is a dreary monotony of plain two and three story frame buildings with accommodations for from two to twelve families, sometimes fronting the street, and sometimes ugly alleys. In most yards the tramp of many feet has prevented the growth of grass although there are exceptions to this. Even where the interiors of the tenements are well

[43] *Ibid.* Pp. 164—177.

[44] *Ibid.* P. 308.

[45] *Ibid.* Pp. 199—200.

kept, hallways are apt to be defaced and uncleanly.[46]

Outside the family, the Portuguese community maintained its identity through the continued use of their native language and their strong affiliation with the Catholic Church. By 1920, Fall River supported six Catholic Churches and fourteen priests.[47] Religion, their solace in times of sorrow, was also the focal point of the happy occasions in their lives. The dreariness and drudgery of everyday life were offset by the joys of birth and community participation in the sacraments of the Church; baptisms, confirmations, and weddings were all occasions for celebration and festivities. With them, when they came to the United States, the Azoreans also brought their tradition of celebrating certain religious holidays. Although these celebrations or *festas* were derived from their religious heritage, much of the activity was secular in nature and took place outside the Church itself. The celebration of the Feast of the Holy Ghost, the major celebration in Azorean communities, usually lasted for several days and provided ample opportunities to dance the *chamarrita* and other traditional dances, to listen to the singing contests between extemporaneous composers, to renew old acquaintances, and to strengthen family ties. The festa concluded on Sunday with a procession through the streets of the city. Led by a band, the procession included groups of men carrying the statues of saints from the church, followed by members of the various religious fraternities. The parade terminated at the church where a High Mass was conducted in Portuguese for the participants and other members of the community. The festa concluded with the serving of a traditional meal of meat and bread to the entire community.

The Blessing of the Fleet in Gloucester and Provincetown, The Feast of the Blessed Sacrament in New Bedford, and the Feast of the Holy Ghost in New Bedford and Fall River were special occasions in the Portuguese communities of New England and were always well attended. Children born in this country were immersed in a Portuguese-speaking culture and learned the traditions of their parents' homeland. Adults reaffirmed their ties to the Portuguese community and maintained contact with members of their extended family. The religious celebrations were also instrumental in maintaining the social networks that existed within the Portuguese communities in the United States and between the United States

[46] *Ibid.* P. 225

[47] *Ibid.* P. 338.

and the Azores. The latest information about friends and conditions in the islands, about new job opportunities, and about the availability of housing circulated as rapidly at the festas as the latest gossip and other small talk. The festas were an important part of the Portuguese community and helped maintain its viability as a recognizable ethnic group — in an area crowded with ethnics. In addition, the celebrations provided a temporary escape from the monotony of day-to-day living.

The Portuguese community lived together, worshipped together and celebrated together. Although this close relationship was instrumental in maintaining the cohesiveness of the community, it effectively delayed the normal acculturation process; many Portuguese immigrants were slow to learn English and other aspects of American culture which could have facilitated upward mobility. A young boy, living in New Bedford at the time later recalled, "I had no opportunity to learn any English, I worked with Portuguese people and lived with Portuguese people all during that time. Even my boss was Portuguese".[48]

Unable to appreciate the economic advantages of education, the immigrants and their children had little chance for advancement in the mills. To improve their economic status, several members of the family had to work; even then their meager resources had to be frugally managed. In many ways, their situation in the United States was not too different from what it had been in the islands, except that here there were many opportunities for employment. Those opportunities for employment continued to attract Portuguese immigrants until they were excluded by restrictive legislation in 1917 and 1921.

In 1900 the 17,885 foreign born Portuguese in Massachusetts were concentrated in six counties. The major concentration was in Bristol County where 63.5 percent of the Portuguese were located. Most were either in Fall River or New Bedford. Middlesex County accounted for 9.7 percent and most of these were in Lowell, a major textile center. The Portuguese were still important in the fishing industry and 6.9 percent of them lived in Barnstable County where Provincetown and Cape Cod were located; another 5.6 percent were in Essex County, the home of the fishing port of Gloucester, and the textile town of Lawrence. Suffolk County, which was almost all encompassed by Boston, contained 6.7 percent and the remaining 3.4 percent were in Plymouth County (*See,* Map 2). By 1910, the

---

[48] Oliver, *Never Backward.* P. 18.

MAP 2

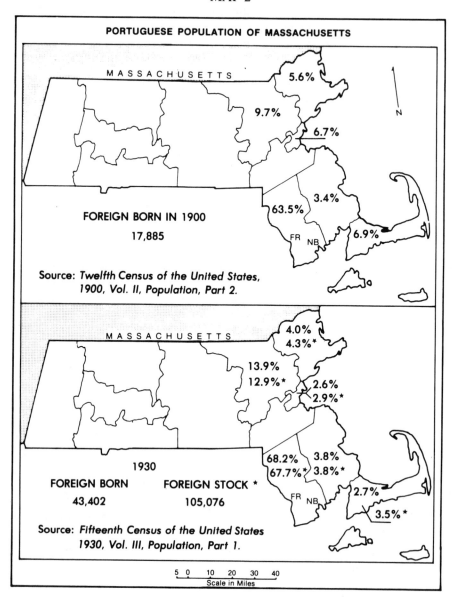

PORTUGUESE POPULATION OF MASSACHUSETTS

MASSACHUSETTS

5.6%

9.7%

6.7%

3.4%

63.5%

6.9%

FR   NB

FOREIGN BORN IN 1900

17,885

Source: *Twelfth Census of the United States,*
1900, Vol. II, Population, Part 2.

MASSACHUSETTS

4.0%
4.3%*

13.9%
12.9%*

2.6%
2.9%*

68.2%   3.8%
67.7%* 3.8%*

2.7%

3.5%*

FR   NB

1930

FOREIGN BORN   FOREIGN STOCK *

43,402   105,076

Source: *Fifteenth Census of the United States*
1930, Vol. III, Population, Part 1.

5 0   10   20   30   40
Scale in Miles

Portuguese population of Massachusetts had more than doubled and in 1920, which was the high point of the second stage of immigration, there were 50,294 foreign born Portuguese in the state.[49] Between 1920 and 1930 the number of foreign born Portuguese in Massachusetts declined by 7,000 but the 43,042 Portuguese immigrants living in the state in 1930 were concentrated in the same six counties where they were found thirty years earlier. The only noticeable change was a slightly greater concentration in both Bristol and Middlesex counties, which were already the leading counties in 1900. In addition to the foreign born population, the Census of 1930 included a category labeled "white foreign stock"; these were immigrants and their children — the first and second generations. In spite of low-paying jobs, high infant mortality rates and difficult living conditions, Massachusetts was home to some 62,000 second generation Portuguese in 1930. Given the nature of the Portuguese community, it is not too surprising that the relative distribution of the 105,076 Portuguese foreign stock in Massachusetts in 1930 was almost identical to the pattern first apparent in the 1900 Census (*See,* Map 2).

Rhode Island, like the neighboring state of Massachusetts, was easy to get to from the Azores and had ample employment opportunities to attract the second wave of Portuguese immigrants. It did not, however, have a substantial Portuguese population in 1870 when only 189 foreign born Portuguese were counted in the entire state. What it did have was proximity to Bristol County, Massachusetts, where more than half of all the Portuguese in Massachusetts were located. Fall River, commonly referred to as the "border city", abutted Newport County, Rhode Island, a rural agricultural area, and was only eighteen miles from Providence, the capital and industrial center of the state. One way in which Rhode Island benefitted from its nearness to Massachusetts was in the number of Portuguese immigrants who "spilled over" into the state from Fall River and New Bedford after 1890. Many of these immigrants ended up in nearby Providence where there was a demand for unskilled laborers. In the early 1900s, Portuguese men in Providence were employed as "longshoremen and deckhands, coal and brick workers, hand operators in oyster and screw companies, and pork packers in meat houses".[50] Portuguese women in Rhode Island, like their counterparts in nearby Massachusetts, commonly worked

[49] *Fourteenth Census of the United States, 1920,* Vol. 3, *Population.* Washington, D.C., 1920.

[50] Susan T. Ferst, "The Immigration and the Settlement of the Portuguese in Providence: 1890 to 1924". Unpublished M.A. Thesis, Brown University, 1972. P. 22.

outside the home; they were mainly employed in lace factories, laundries and cotton mills.[51]

The urban pattern of life for Portuguese immigrants in Providence was similar to that in Fall River and New Bedford. New arrivals joined relatives or friends already living in the city or stayed in lodging houses with other Portuguese speaking immigrants. They depended heavily upon informal contacts with friends and relatives to secure employment. "Because most jobs came through unofficial middlemen, the type and place of employment usually followed residential and family patterns".[52] The existence of a strong social network, which played such an important role in obtaining employment and housing, was instrumental in reinforcing local community ties and discouraging integration with non-Portuguese in the community. Within their tight-knit community, which consisted primarily of Azoreans from the islands of São Miguel and Faial, they shared the social customs common to their homeland and maintained a very high degree of intermarriage; it was not uncommon for marriage partners to be from the same hometown in the Azores.[53] The new immigrants in Providence, not unlike their countrymen in Fall River and New Bedford, relied almost exclusively upon "their fellow Portuguese for advice, money, and ethnic support because of their tendencies to group together and to shun public charity".[54]

For many Azoreans toiling as unskilled laborers in the textile mills of New England, a small farm of their own was a dream to be nurtured and a goal to work toward. For most it remained just that, a dream never quite attained, and they and their offspring made the permanent transition from rural folk to urban industrial workers. Others, either more fortunate or more determined, started out in the mills but were able to save enough money to get them started in farming. They bought small farms and took up market gardening and dairying.[55] More typically, for those who eventually ended up as independent farmers, was the slow progression from farm laborer, to tenant, to owner of a mortgaged farm, and finally to the

[51] *Ibid.* P. 23.

[52] *Ibid.* P. 25.

[53] *Ibid.* Pp. 25—32.

[54] *Ibid.* P. 32.

[55] Leo Pap, *Portuguese American Speech: An Outline of Speech Conditions Among the Portuguese Immigrants in New England and Elsewhere in the United States.* N. Y., 1949. P. 13

envied position of possessing a clear title to their own farm.[56] Every change in status was accompanied by deprivation and hard work and it was only after they successfully made the transition from farm laborer to owner that they were occasionally able to indulge in anything more than the most basic necessities of life.

While Portuguese immigrants in Fall River and New Bedford worked in the mills and dreamed of owning a farm, many of the farmers in nearby Newport County, and elsewhere in New England, saw the new employment possibilities and the increasing amenities of urban living as a decided improvement over their traditional rural life and started moving to the cities. Behind them they left abandoned or idle farms which they were only too happy to rent and sell to the would-be farmers from the Azores. Portsmouth, Rhode Island, a rural farming community about twelve miles southwest of Fall River, was one of several communities where Portuguese immigrants were successful in getting back to the land. Prior to 1890 there were few Portuguese in Portsmouth; thirty years later they comprised almost half of the community's population — some 1,177 out of a total population of 2,590. Unlike Fall River, where there were a number of other ethnic groups competing for jobs and housing, the Portuguese constituted virtually the entire foreign element in Portsmouth.[57]

Getting a farm was one thing, making it support a family and pay for itself was something else. Azoreans were not unaccustomed to hard work and niggardly rewards from the soil, but they were forced to employ all the agricultural know-how they had learned in their homeland to make the farmlands of Rhode Island support them.

> They are in the fields as long as it is light and employ the labor of every member of their families old enough to wield a hoe. Being in addition exceedingly frugal, and understanding intensive farming, they are successful on New England farms where the native farmer has either failed or found more lucrative employment in the city. Their economic success is often, however, at the expense of the health and happiness of wives and children, and it spells hard work with little recreation for the whole family.[58]

[56] Taft, *Two Portuguese Communities in New England.* P. 258.

[57] *Ibid.* Pp. 196—202.

[58] *Ibid.* P. 255.

In contrast to life in the nearby mill towns, where Portuguese immigrants were surrounded by their countrymen, life for the newcomer to Portsmouth was one of isolation. Living conditions, however, were worse in the country than they were in the cities. "Many of the houses are old and poorly equipped and most are, of course, lacking in modern conveniences, but these conditions are the typical rural situation".[59] Economic survival dictated hard work by every member of the family and a willingness to live at a low standard of living and do without many of the things that others in American society considered essentials. They persevered, however, and the number of land-owning versus land-renting Portuguese slowly increased. Portsmouth, for example, witnessed an increase in Portuguese land owners from only one in 1885 to 84 in 1920. The determination and industriousness of the Portuguese soon earned them a reputation as first class farmers who could make the land produce when no one else could. Recognition of their farming ability was epitomized in a saying which became common in New England in the early part of the 20th century: "If you want to see a potato grow, you have to speak to it in Portuguese". As the years passed they were able to make noticeable economic progress, but, as in the mill towns, that progress was achieved through considerable personal sacrifice: long hours of hard work, deprivation from all but the most basic necessities, minimal exposure to education for their children and little contact with the larger American society. The Portuguese who succeeded in agriculture, however, won the respect of even their most severe critics; as one of them admitted, "As a people willing to work in abandoned farms and able to make a living from them, the Portuguese seem to be a real asset".[60]

Whatever their occupation, the Portuguese population of Rhode Island steadily increased after 1890. In 1900 there were 2,545 foreign born Portuguese in the state: 53.7 percent of them resided in Providence County and worked as unskilled labor in the capital city; 32.4 percent lived in rural Newport County; and 10.6 percent in Bristol County (*See,* Map 3). In the next ten years, the Portuguese population increased two and a half times; the Census of 1910 recorded 6,571 foreign born Portuguese living in Rhode Island.[61] New Portuguese immigrants continued to locate in the state until the restrictive legislation of the mid-1920s effectively curtailed the flow of immigrants to the entire country. The Census of 1930 enumerated

[59] *Ibid.* P. 228.

[60] *Ibid.* P. 349.

[61] *Thirteenth Census of the United States, 1910,* Vol. 2, *Population. Washington, D.C. 1910.*

MAP 3

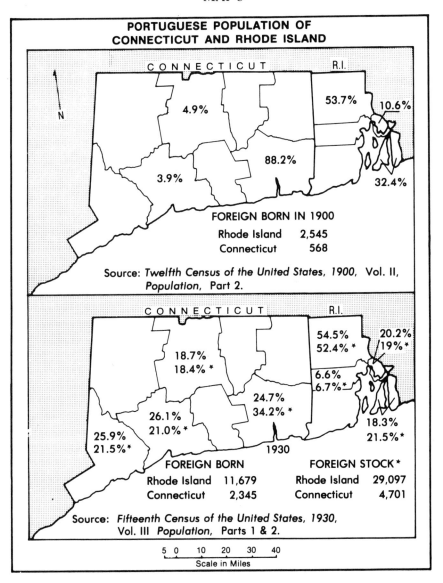

PORTUGUESE POPULATION OF
CONNECTICUT AND RHODE ISLAND

CONNECTICUT   R.I.

N

4.9%   53.7%   10.6%

88.2%

3.9%   32.4%

FOREIGN BORN IN 1900

Rhode Island   2,545
Connecticut   568

Source: *Twelfth Census of the United States, 1900,* Vol. II,
Population, Part 2.

CONNECTICUT   R.I.

54.5%   20.2%
52.4% *   19% *

18.7%
18.4% *

6.6%
6.7% *

24.7%
34.2% *

26.1%
21.0% *

18.3%
25.9%   21.5% *
21.5% *   1930

FOREIGN BORN   FOREIGN STOCK *

Rhode Island   11,679   Rhode Island   29,097
Connecticut   2,345   Connecticut   4,701

Source: *Fifteenth Census of the United States, 1930,*
Vol. III *Population,* Parts 1 & 2.

5 0   10   20   30   40
Scale in Miles

29,097 Portuguese foreign stock in Rhode Island; 11,679 were foreign born and the other 17,418 were their offspring. The major change in the distribution of Portuguese in Rhode Island, both foreign born and their offspring, between 1900 and 1930 was the continued attraction of urban jobs in the Providence area. The growth of the Providence urban area was also reflected in the increase of Portuguese in Bristol County to 20.2 percent and in Kent County, which appears for the first time, with 6.6 percent of the foreign born in 1930. Newport County continued to experience an absolute increase in its Portuguese population but its relative percentage, statewide, declined to 18.3 percent in 1930 (*See,* Map 3).

In many ways Connecticut was similar to Rhode Island: it was as close as either Massachusetts or Rhode Island to the Azores, although not quite so accessible; there were jobs for unskilled laborers in the state's developing industries; and, it had a small, 221 individuals, foreign born Portuguese population in 1870. The similarities ended there. Most importantly, it did not share Rhode Island's proximity to a large Portuguese immigrant population. New London, known as the Whaling City in Connecticut, was comparable to New Bedford in that most of the Portuguese in Connecticut in 1870 were there as a result of whaling. Between 1870 and 1900 most of the Portuguese immigrants that went to Connecticut joined friends or relatives already living there. In 1900, then, the major concentration of Portuguese in Connecticut was in New London County where the former whaling port of New London was located. Although 88 percent of the Portuguese in Connecticut were in New London County, there were only 568 foreign born Portuguese in the entire state. Five percent of those were in Hartford County, the major industrial center of the state, and another four percent were in New Haven County which was the location of both the port of New Haven and the industrial city of Meriden (*See,* Map 3).

Virtually all of the increase in Portuguese immigration into Connecticut between 1900 and 1930 was to the industrial centers of the state. The total Portuguese population of New London County increased only slightly while the county's percentage of the state total dropped from 88.2 percent in 1900 to 24.7 percent in 1930. Other noticeable changes were in Fairfield County which accounted for 25.9 percent of the state's foreign born Portuguese population in 1930 and New Haven and Hartford Counties which increased to 26.1 percent and 18.7 percent respectively (*See,* Map 3).

Although the immigration process was virtually identical for Azoreans who settled on the east and west coasts, there was a noticeable difference in the environment in which they found themselves. The east coast of the United States was already well settled when the main flow of Portuguese immigrants arrived and, as a consequence, the majority of the Azoreans who settled there had little choice but to make a rapid transition from their former rural lifestyle to a new urban-industrial way of life. The west coast was far removed from the economic center of the nation at the turn of the century and the opportunities and experiences which the new immigrants encountered there were decidedly different from those which occurred in New England at that time. Those differences have been reflected in the Portuguese population of the United States ever since.

Chapter III

California and Hawaii: Life in the West

Contrary to popular mythology, California was not an unknown land that sprang into existence with the discovery of gold in 1848 and the subsequent invasion by the '49ers. Although Joao Cabrilho, a Portuguese captain, is credited with discovering California for the Europeans in 1542, he was under the employ of the Spanish crown. Furthermore, another three hundred years elapsed before the first permanent Portuguese settler arrived in California. Part of the Spanish Empire until 1822, when Mexico gained its independence, only the coastal area of California was occupied by these would-be *conquistadores.* Unable to find large concentrations of either Indians or wealth they turned their interest to grazing cattle on the extensive holdings of natural range. Even so, California was not unknown to the inhabitants of the east coast of the United States. Contraband fur traders from Massachusetts had frequented the coast of California since before the turn of the 19th century. After Mexico gained its independence, it was merchant seamen out of Massachusetts who traded their merchandise for California cowhides in the 1830s and '40s, so vividly described by John Henry Dana in *Two Years Before the Mast .*[62] In his trip to California (1834—36), Dana encountered "Massachusetts men established all along the Coast, from a one-eyed Fall River whaleman tending bar in a San Diego *pulperia,* to Thomas O. Larkin, the merchant prince of Monterey".[63] Those cowhides, known as California cartwheels, helped supply the needed raw

[62] John Henry Dana, *Two Years Before the Mast: A Personal Narrative of Life at Sea.* New York, 1936.

[63] Morison, *The Maritime History of Massachusetts.* P. 267.

materials for the New England shoe factories in the 19th century. After the New Bedford whalers started working the Pacific whaling grounds in the late 1830s, they frequently stopped along the California coast for fresh beef.

All in all, there had been considerable contact between California and New England prior to 1849, and many a sailor, who successfully jumped ship to escape intolerable conditions on board, had a change of heart after a few years in this new land and took the first opportunity to depart. In the early part of the 19th century, California could not have been an overly attractive place to stay: settlements were small, few and far between; isolated as they were from Mexico, the occupants were forced to be self-sufficient in almost everything; and, the local economy provided little, other than cowhides, to exchange with the occasional merchant ship. The first record of a permanent Portuguese resident was that of Antonio José Rocha, who, along with nine other men, deserted an English ship in Monterey in 1815. Foreigners were not welcome in California at that time and the other nine deserters were returned to their ship. Rocha, skilled as a carpenter and blacksmith, was also a Catholic of Latin heritage and, for whatever reasons, was not returned to his ship. He eventually made his way to the Los Angeles area, married and settled there.[64] One deserter, however, hardly constitutes a migration, and the total number of foreigners living in California increased very slowly. By 1830, about 150 foreigners were living in the area and only five of those were Portuguese; it was not until Antonio Silva arrived in 1840, that the first Portuguese whaler deserted his ship to take up life in California.[65]

Given the right motivation, conditions can change rapidly, even in the 1840s; when word of the California gold strike reached New England there were many sea captains there already experienced in sailing around Cape Horn and up the west coast of North America. The rush was on! The first outpouring from the east coast consisted of men anxious to be first in the gold fields. "The gold fever drained Nantucket of one-quarter of its voting population in nine months. In the same period, eight hundred men left New Bedford for the mines". [66]

Some of the first Portuguese immigrants to California were among those sailing from New Bedford and Nantucket. Sailing as a

[64] John Walton, *A Historical Study of the Portuguese in California*. San Francisco, 1972. Pp. 30—46.

[65] *Ibid.* Pp. 46—48.

[66] Morison, *The Maritime History of Massachusetts.* P. 333.

passenger to California, while certainly the most desirable way to travel, was also the most expensive. The crew on these sailing ships arrived in California at the same time the passengers did, and although the trip was not so pleasant, it was equally fast. The initial rush to find gold was followed by a determined effort on the part of those who remained at home to share in this new found wealth. There was an immediate need for all kinds of food and merchandise to outfit these argonauts departing daily from San Francisco and Sacramento. The merchants of New England were quick to respond. Again ships and sailors were needed to get the cargo to California quickly. For many, it was a one-way trip. "In July 1850, there were 512 abandoned vessels lying in front of the city of San Francisco, some with unloaded cargoes".[67] Most of the Portuguese who availed themselves of the slow moving whalers missed the frenzied rush to be first, but there was still gold to be found when they arrived. As they soon learned, though, finding gold was not an easy task.

The geography of California was not well known in the 1840s and what many expected would be a relatively quick trip to pick up gold nuggets lying on the ground was not to be. Instead, they discovered that it was a long journey in 1849 from San Francisco to the Mother Lode, by boat, horse or afoot, and even longer to the Klamath Mountains at the north end of the Sacramento Valley. The would-be miner without sufficient resources to purchase the necessary equipment and supplies to sustain him in his search had little chance of success and many of the new arrivals were acutely short of capital. As it turned out, getting to the gold fields was the easiest part of being a gold miner. Once there, the real problems surfaced: difficulty in obtaining food (when it was available it was frequently poor in quality and always exorbitantly priced); miserable living conditions (many miners had only rudimentary shelters that offered little protection from the harsh winter weather in the Sierra Nevada Mountains); little, if any, medical treatment available (there was little hope for the unfortunate miner who became seriously ill or injured); and the constant threat of claim jumpers or robbers (finding gold was one thing, getting home with it was another). Many '49ers became discouraged after a year or two and departed from the gold fields; those that were financially able frequently returned home, the rest sought a way to earn a living.

How many Portuguese there were in California in 1850 and whether or not they were engaged in mining is not precisely

---

[67] Walton, *A Historical Study of the Portuguese in California.* P. 51

known. The first official census of California was taken in 1850 under, admittedly, adverse conditions. The population was migratory and transient and the result was, at best, a rough estimate. One hundred and nine Portuguese were enumerated in that census out of a total population of 92,597.[68] The Portuguese first began to arrive in California, in any appreciable numbers, in the 1850s; by 1860, when the next official census was conducted, the state's population had increased to 379,994 and 1,580 were listed as being born in either Portugal or the Atlantic Islands.[69] No doubt most of them were attracted to California by the gold rush; the manuscript census for that year reveals that there were 844 Portuguese miners scattered around the gold fields of California. The majority went to the Mother Lode county east of Sacramento, but a group of them wound up in the extreme northern part of the state in Hawkinsville, "the only Portuguese-dominated mining settlement (that) persisted throughout the latter part of the nineteenth century".[70] Hawkinsville, never much more than a collection of miners' shacks, was gradually supplanted by its larger neighbor Yreka, but as late as 1880 it still had 313 inhabitants and 175 of them were Portuguese. The early, labor intensive, days of placer mining, where alluvial deposits were panned to find particles of gold washed down from higher elevations, gradually gave way to more capital intensive, hard rock mining which involved following a vein of gold-bearing quartz into the side of a mountain by sinking shafts or blasting tunnels. The resulting ore had to be crushed in a stamp mill to separate the gold from the quartz and bedrock. Mining companies were better able to support the costs involved in both hard rock and hydraulic mining, where entire hillsides were washed away with high pressure streams of water; for the individual miner the choice increasingly came down to working for a large mining corporation for wages or getting out of mining. Many took the latter alternative.

In many ways the life of a gold miner was not unlike that of a whaler; the hours were long, the work was hard and the rewards uncertain. Disappointed miners began abandoning the mining fields in the early 1850s and turning to other occupations; the natural inclination was to employ whatever skills and experiences an individual already possessed. A

[68] Allyn C. Loosley, "Foreign Born Population of California". Unpublished M.A. Thesis, Univ. of California, Berkeley, 1927. P. 5.

[69] *Eighth Census of the United States, 1860.* Vol. I.

[70] Alvin Graves, "Immigrants in Agriculture: The Portuguese Californians, 1850–1970s". Unpublished Ph.D. dissertation, Univ. of California, Los Angeles, 1977. P. 49.

number of Portuguese turned back to the sea. As early as 1854, some of these former whalers decided to try their luck in California waters. In 1854, a San Francisco newspaper reported, "A number of Portuguese fishermen have caught twenty-four whales of all kinds in the bay of Monterey since April last".[71] During the next thirty years, Portuguese whalers from the Azores established shore whaling stations at a number of points along the California coast from Crescent City, near the Oregon border, to San Diego (*See*, Map 4). Many of these whaling stations resembled a coastal village in the Azores,

> Scattered around the foothills, which come to the water's edge, are the nearby whitewashed cabins of the whalers, nearly all of whom are Portuguese, from the Azores or Western Islands of the Atlantic. They have their families with them, and keep a pig, sheep, goat, or cow, prowling around the premises; these, with a small garden-patch, yielding principally corn and pumpkins, make up the general picture of the hamlet...".[72]

These whalers pursued the gray whales that annually migrate in the winter from the Arctic waters around Alaska to the mating and calving grounds off Baja California and then back again in the spring. Their habit of migrating along the coastline made them an easy target for exploitation by shore whalers The life of a whaling station depended upon how successful the men were; some were very short lived while others were in more or less continuous operation until shore whaling was finally abandoned in the 1880s. Some stations were well organized commercial operations, others consisted of a few fishermen who would get together and decide to try their luck at whaling during the slack fishing seasons, or men who were farmers part of the year and whalers in the winter and spring.[73] Almost all of the shore whalers, however, were Azoreans and occasionally the same men were involved in shore whaling at several different locations.

> Captain Frank Anderson, who is now said to be the most experienced whaling captain on the coast, is a native of the Azores Islands, his Portuguese name having been dropped on naturalization in the United

[71] Edwin C. Starks, *A History of California Shore Whaling.* Sacramento, 1922. P. 17.

[72] Scammon, *The Marine Mammals of the North-Western Coast of North America.* P. 250.

[73] Starks, *A History of California Shore Whaling.* P. 20.

MAP 4

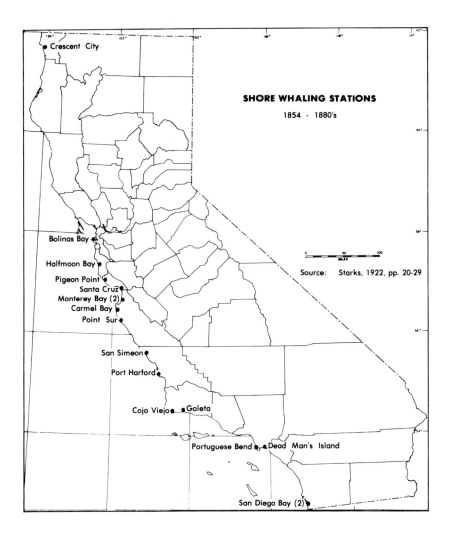

Crescent City

SHORE WHALING STATIONS

1854 - 1880's

Source: Starks, 1922, pp. 20-29

Bolinas Bay

Halfmoon Bay

Pigeon Point

Santa Cruz

Monterey Bay (2)

Carmel Bay

Point Sur

San Simeon

Port Harford

Cojo Viejo   Goleta

Portuguese Bend   Dead Man's Island

San Diego Bay (2)

States, as is the general custom among the natives of the Azores. He was first a whaler on ships from New Bedford, then came to California in 1866, and since 1873 he has had charge of whaling camps as captain. He was at San Luis Obispo until 1874, at Portuguese Bend till 1877, and at Pigeon Point until 1879, when he with his entire company moved to Cojo Viejo.[74]

The constant over-exploitation of the whale population, both along the coast and in deep water, inevitably led to a decline in the catch. The combination of fewer whales, difficulty in securing seamen, and increased competition from petroleum products gradually changed the image of the whaling industry, after about 1870, from a very profitable enterprise to a very risky one. Many whalers were forced to turn to other occupations for their livelihood. In California, commercial agriculture was a likely occupation for many immigrants. In contrast to the east coast of the United States, most of the land suitable for cultivation in California was settled in the last half of the 19th century. For the individual with a knowledge of farming and the inclination to use it, the possibilities seemed unlimited. Although most of the land suitable for agriculture was already privately owned, it was not being farmed intensively. Much of the land in California was being utilized to graze cattle, an extensive system of land use, but the large landholdings needed to support a family in such a system were unnecessary and, in fact, wasteful in the eyes of the Portuguese and other immigrants who were accustomed to making do with less.

Confident that they could earn a living on a relatively small piece of land and encouraged by the success of their countrymen who had taken up farming when most other newcomers were still searching for gold, Portuguese immigrants increasingly turned to agriculture for a livelihood. Converting the dream of being an independent farmer into reality, however, was seldom an easy task. Almost all of the Portuguese arrived in California with little or no money; in its place they brought a willingness to work and endure hardships and personal sacrifice to achieve their goals. Most of those who ended up as independent farmers slowly progressed from working for wages to tenant farming and eventually to private ownership of the land they tilled. The process usually took several years.[75]

---

[74] George Brown Goode, *The Fisheries and Fishery Industry of the United States,* Vol. V, Part II. P. 55.

[75] U.S. Congress, "Portuguese Farmers About San Leandro, California". In *Immigrant Farmers*

The areas around San Francisco Bay, the arrival and departure point for the passengers and cargo bound for California, and Sacramento, the *entrepôt* to the gold fields, were rapidly settled by people seeking an alternative to an uncertain life searching for gold. In the Census of 1860, one in every four Portuguese men listed his occupation as some type of agricultural activity. Alameda and Contra Costa, the two counties directly across the bay from San Francisco, had the greatest concentration of Portuguese, followed by the area around Sacramento in Yolo and Sacramento counties.[76] Many of the Portuguese followed the time-honored tradition of working as agricultural laborers until they could accumulate enough money to rent and then eventually buy their own small farm. Utilizing the intensive farming techniques of their homeland, they raised fruit and vegetables which found a ready market in the nearby cities.

The area just north of San Francisco, Marin County, is lacking in flat land suited for cultivation, but possesses ideal conditions for raising livestock. It soon became known for its dairy farms, many of them specializing in producing butter. Some of the large landowners quickly discovered they could make better use of their holdings by dividing them into a number of small farms operated by tenant farmers on a share basis. The owner provided the fenced land, necessary buildings and cows while the tenant provided:

> the dairy utensils, the needed horses and wagons, the furniture for the house, the farm implements, and the necessary labor. The tenant pays to the owner twenty-seven dollars and a half per annum for each cow, and agrees to take the best care of the stock and of all parts of the farm; to make the necessary repairs, and to raise for the owner annually one-fifth as many calves as he keeps cows, the remainder of the calves being killed and fed to the pigs. He agrees also to sell nothing but butter and hogs from the farm, the hogs being entirely the tenant's property.[77]

---

in the Western States. Senate Report of the U.S. Immigration Commission, Vol. 24, Pt.II. U.S. Government Printing Office, 1911. Chap. XIV. P. 491.

[76] Graves, "Immigrants in Agriculture", Pp. 50—51.

[77] Charles Nordhoff, *Northern California, Oregon, and the Sandwich Islands.* New York, 1874. P. 180.

To take over one of these dairy farms in 1870, a tenant needed about $2,000 and experience raising cows and pigs; the experience they had — the capital they acquired. A number of Portuguese became tenant dairy farmers. For those lacking the capital to operate a dairy farm themselves, there were always jobs available as hired hands. "The milkers and farm hands receive thirty dollars per month and 'found', and good milkers are in constant demand".[78] Gradually, a pattern of movement evolved among Portuguese dairymen: young men would work as milkers on tenant farms operated by other Portuguese, not infrequently a relative or former acquaintance, until they could accumulate enough money to become a tenant farmer themselves; at the same time, the tenant farmers were working to acquire enough capital to buy their own herd and dairy farm. The tenant farms of the San Francisco Bay area became a way-station for many Portuguese who later became dairy farmers in the Central Valley of California.

As a destination for Portuguese immigrants after 1870, California appeared, at first glance, to be only slightly more attractive than Hawaii: the gold rush fever was subsiding; there was no industrial development comparable to the textile mills of New England; and, to get to California required a tiring cross-country trip from the east coast. In spite of its apparent shortcomings, the state was home to 3,435 foreign born Portuguese in 1870, forty percent of the total Portuguese population of the United States, and the attraction of friends and family overshadowed all other considerations for the new immigrants. In addition, good agricultural land was still available in California.

In the early 1870s, the Portuguese in Alameda County, directly across the bay from San Francisco, were noted as being "amongst the most thriving portion of our population, occupying as they do, small farms of the best land and growing vegetables and fruit".[79] With the largest concentration of people in the state at that time, the San Francisco Bay area provided a ready market for the agricultural produce of the region. Proximity to this market increased the value of bay area land, but the Portuguese, certain that good agricultural land would pay for itself, were willing to pay high prices for small parcels. So much so, that a writer in Alameda County was prompted to note, with tongue in cheek, "A Portuguese advancing toward your premises for the purpose of negotiating a purchase, adds much

[78] *Ibid.* P. 181.

[79] William Halley, *The Centennial Year Book of Alameda County, California.* Oakland, 1876. Pp. 292–293.

greater enhancement to its value than the assurances of having a railroad pass through your veranda".[80]

As new immigrants continued to buy land in and around San Leandro, a farming community in Alameda County, it gradually became known as the Portuguese center in the bay area. In contrast to the size of traditional California landholdings, most Portuguese farms were quite small. In 1908, the United States Immigration Commission interviewed Portuguese farmers in San Leandro as part of their *Immigrant Farmers in the Western States* study and found the average Portuguese farm holding was 46.6 acres while the median farm size was 12.5 acres.[81] Like many other farmers in the United States at that time, the Portuguese in San Leandro produced almost all of their own food supply. They all kept gardens and fruit trees, almost all had a few milk cows which furnished milk and butter, and over half of them kept swine to help provide part of their meat. One noteworthy difference that the study found between Portuguese and American farmers was that "the former employ their countrymen practically to the exclusion of other races whether as regular or as temporary hands".[82] The process whereby Portuguese immigrants settled in San Leandro and gradually converted it into a Portuguese community was vividly described by one of the characters in Jack London's novel, *The Valley of the Moon:*

> Forty years ago Silva came from the Azores. Went sheep-herdin' in the mountains for a couple of years, then blew in to San Leandro. These five acres was the first land he leased. That was the beginnin'. Then he began leasin' by the hundreds of acres, an' by the hundred-an'-sixties. An' his sisters an' his uncles an' his aunts begun pourin' in from the Azores — they're all related there, you know; an' pretty soon San Leandro was a regular Porchugeeze settlement.[83]

Successful farming in California during the latter part of the 19th century required a knowledge of agricultural practices, good land and a market for the produce. Being able to make the land produce was a

[80] *Ibid.* P. 198.

[81] *Immigrant Farmers in the Western States.* P. 490.

[82] *Ibid.* Pp. 490—491.

[83] Jack London, *The Valley of the Moon.* New York, 1914.

necessity instilled in Azoreans from early childhood; to survive in their homeland they had to learn how to maximize production from every bit of land. It was only natural that Portuguese immigrants applied that same knowledge and determination to farming in California.

> It hurts a Portuguese to waste an inch of land. He'll buy the best land out of doors — knows the best when he sees it too — and will pay a top price without question or flinching; but after he gets it he wants every inch of it to be working for him, night and day, every minute of the growing season.
> One of these town orchards in San Leandro has currants between the orchard rows, beans between the currant rows, a row of beans close on each side of the trees, and beans from the end of the rows to the wheeltracks in the street. Not satisfied with this degree of intensiveness and interplanting, the owner doubled the number of rows in the space or corner where his private sidewalk joined the public street.[84]

By 1880, when the Portuguese foreign born in California numbered 7,990, well over sixty percent were working as farmers or farm laborers and more than seventy percent of them were living in the Central Coast area.[85] While the Central Coast, which stretches from San Luis Obispo County in the south to Sonoma County in the north, was home for more than seventy percent of all Portuguese in California, sixty percent of the total were concentrated in the San Francisco—Oakland Bay Area and predominantly engaged in agricultural activities of one type or another. Although the other thirty percent were spread around the state, they too tended to be concentrated in a relatively small number of locations and occupations. The Sacramento Valley, which is in the northern third of the Central Valley, and particularly the area in the vicinity of Sacramento, accounted for about eleven percent of the total Portuguese population with most of the working population engaged in agriculture; some were also occupied in fishing and urban oriented jobs in the city. Gold mining was still an important occupation for a small number of Portuguese immigrants in 1880; the largest concentrations were located in the major mining centers

---

[84] Forest Crissey, *Where Opportunity Knocks Twice*. Chicago, 1914. Pp. 74—75.

[85] Graves, "Immigrants in Agriculture". Pp. 52—53.

in the Sierra Nevada Mountains while a lesser number could still be found in the northern part of the state. The San Joaquin Valley, which is in the southern two-thirds of the Central Valley, was notable for the number of Portuguese sheep raisers and tenders as well as agriculturalists. Another minor concentration was located in Mendocino County along the North coast where they worked in the forestry industries. Southern California had the fewest Portuguese in 1880, with a small community of former shore-whalers living in the Los Angeles area and an active whaling group in Santa Barbara County.[86] Over half of all the Portuguese in the United States were living in California in 1880;[87] these new immigrants overwhelmingly chose agriculture as an occupation and Alameda County and the surrounding bay area as their preferred residential location.

Between 1880 and 1900 the number of foreign born Portuguese in California almost doubled, but the general locational pattern changed only slightly during the twenty years. Thirty-two percent of the 15,583 foreign born Portuguese living in California in 1900 could be found in Alameda County. Contra Costa County, on the north side of Alameda County, and Santa Clara County, on the south side, each accounted for another seven percent of the Portuguese immigrants, while Marin County, north of San Francisco, retained 5.2 percent and San Francisco County 3.9 percent. Together those five bay area counties were home to fifty-five percent of all the foreign born Portuguese in California in 1900 and, as Map 5 illustrates, were at the core of a predominantly coastal pattern of distribution concentrated between Marin County in the north and San Luis Obispo County in the south.

The tempo of out-migration from the Azores reached its peak between 1890 and 1920 as the inhabitants reluctantly fled from the difficult life in their homeland. The Portuguese population of the Hawaiian Islands and the east coast also increased dramatically and California's percentage of the United States' total stabilized at about one-third; in 1900 the 15,583 foreign born Portuguese in California represented 32.4 percent of the nation's total. California's population of Portuguese immigrants doubled again by 1920 when they numbered 33,025.[88] After 1920 new and more restrictive immigration laws, together with worsening economic conditions

[86] *Ibid.* Pp. 58—62.

[87] *Ibid.* P.93.

[88] *Fourteenth Census of the United States, 1920,* Vol. 3, *Population.*

for United States farmers, brought new immigration to a virtual standstill and provided the necessary incentive for a substantial return migration of disenchanted immigrants. At the close of the second stage of migration in 1930, California's foreign born Portuguese population totaled 35,395 and their offspring numbered another 63,799; together they comprised a Portuguese population of 99,194. Those 35,395 foreign born Portuguese constituted 32.4 percent of the nation's total — the exact same percentage found in the state in 1900. Within California, however, a major change had occurred in the location and occupation of the Portuguese population in the course of thirty years. While Alameda County still represented the single largest concentration of Portuguese in the state, its share had declined to 25.6 percent. More importantly, the general focus of Portuguese settlement had shifted away from the Central Coast and to the Central Valley of California. An eight-county area in the Central Valley, consisting of Solano and Sacramento on the north end, King and Tulare on the south, and the four counties in between, which accounted for slightly more than ten percent of the foreign born Portuguese population in 1900 when the state's total was 15,583, now represented thirty-five percent of the state's 35,395 Portuguese immigrants (*See,* Map 5).

The move toward the Central Valley after 1900 was at least partially motivated by the perceived opportunities there for dairymen. Most of the early Portuguese dairymen started out in Marin County, north of San Francisco, and gradually made the transition from milker to tenant farmer to owner. After the turn of the century sheep raising declined in the Central Valley as range land was divided up by irrigation canals; some of the Portuguese who had formerly tended sheep turned to dairy cows and irrigated pasture.[89] To help milk the cows and run the dairies these Portuguese dairymen hired other Portuguese and encouraged relatives and friends from the Azores to join them; after a few years of milking cows and saving their money, many of these immigrants started their own dairies and, in turn, sent for more immigrants to join them. This self-perpetuating sytem reinforced the ties which existed between the immigrant population in California and the Azores by providing both destination and employment for friends and relatives anxious to leave the Azores, by furnishing a continuing supply of new labor for the expanding dairy industry, and by creating a growing class of entrepreneurs anxious to get started with their own dairy.

[89] Crissey, *Where Opportunity Knocks Twice.* Pp. 68—71.

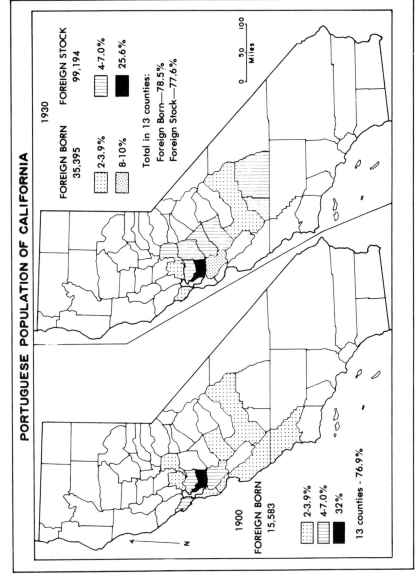

MAP 5

PORTUGUESE POPULATION OF CALIFORNIA

In many ways the dairy industry was ideally suited for the Portuguese immigrants. Although they were poorly educated and had little knowledge of tools and machinery, they were skilled in raising and caring for livestock. Their inability to speak English made little difference in the daily life of running a dairy; tied to the farm by the necessity of milking the animals both morning and night, they seldom needed to communicate with anyone other than hired hands, who inevitably were Portuguese themselves, and the cows, who produced milk regardless of what language the dairymen spoke. In addition, the initial investment needed to start a dairy was minimal; other than the cows themselves, the necessary facilities could be rented or worked on a share basis until such time as enough land could be purchased to establish an owner-operated dairy. The dairy industry expanded rapidly in the Central Valley after 1910 and the initial success of Portuguese dairymen encouraged others to join them. In 1923 eighty-five percent of the dairymen in Merced and Stanislaus Counties were reported to be Portuguese and by 1930 they were well established throughout the San Joaquin Valley dairy industry.[90]

The overwhelming success of Portuguese immigrants in the California dairy industry should not overshadow the fact that while many succeeded, many also failed. The day-to-day life of running a dairy, like any other business, was filled with challenges and difficulties. Some rose to the occasion, while others were not so fortunate. As one Portuguese dairy farmer's wife recalled,

> My husband had five or six milkers — all Portuguese — working on the dairy. When milking machines were introduced no one knew how to use them and they left them on the cows too long and ruined some of the cows. When the government started inspecting cows for T.B., in 1937, they took almost all of our cows — milkers and dry stock too — we were left with only eighteen cows. Everyone was so nervous, no one knew what to do. Each milker had only one or two cows to milk. It was a very serious time. We had to start building a new herd. We bought ten big holsteins and the first one kicked a milking machine all apart — she had never had a machine on her

---

[90] Graves, "Immigrants in Agriculture". P. 120.

before. It took a long time to try to rebuild the herd. A lot of dairies went out of business then.[91]

Following World War I high wages offered for milkers attracted a number of Dutch and Portuguese immigrants to the dairy farms in the Los Angeles area. In the process of making the transition from milker to owner they introduced an entirely new concept into the dairy industry of southern California. Unable to purchase large land holdings to provide extensive pasture for their cattle, they kept them in corrals, as they had in their homeland, and brought feed to them. It soon became apparent that dairying on small units of land, based on a system of corral feeding, was both feasible and profitable.[92] This new technique of corral feeding, or dry-lot dairying as it came to be known, was rapidly copied by other dairy operators and by 1935, virtually the entire southern Los Angeles milkshed had been transformed into dry-lot dairying.[93] Portuguese dairymen eventually dominated the dairy industry in the San Joaquin Valley and became so associated with dairying throughout the state that the words "Portuguese" and "dairy farmer" became almost synonomous.

The Central Valley of California also offered ample opportunities for the would-be farmer and the Portuguese responded to the challenge in a variety of ways. In 1888 John Avila introduced the sweet potato into the Atwater area of Merced County; it became a major commercial crop and he became known as the "father of the sweet potato industry".[94] By the beginning of the second decade of this century, Portuguese farmers were noted growing strawberries near Merced, cherry orchards and asparagus in Stockton, sweet potatoes and pumpkins in an orchard in Oakdale, and lima beans in Ventura.[95] "As practical farmers, the Portuguese of the Pacific Coast — who were almost exclusively from the islands of the Azores — have few peers".[96] The most difficult obstacle to overcome for these immigrant farmers was acquiring enough land to enable them to become more than just

[91] Interview with Maria B. Diniz in Patterson, California, on Nov. 25, 1978.

[92] John G. Gielding, "Dairying in the Los Angeles Milkshed: Factors Affecting Character and Location". Unpublished Ph.D. dissertation, Univ. of California at Los Angeles. P. 32.

[93] *Ibid.* P. 69.

[94] Manoel da Silveira Cardozo, *The Portuguese in America 590 B.C. — 1974.* New York, 1976. P. 37.

[95] Crissey, *Where Opportunity Knocks Twice.* Pp. 78—81.

[96] *Ibid.* P. 59.

subsistence farmers. Working someone else's land on a share basis or being a tenant farmer was the easiest way to start but it offered little security. Every farmer wanted to own his own land, but it was not easy to accomplish. Looking back, one farmer's wife still remembered the constant struggle to become an independent farmer.

> I lived in Stevenson for eleven months after I got married then my husband's partner wanted to sell out and return to the old country. They sold out. My husband looked all over for a piece of ground. He finally found 20 acres here in Patterson (Stanislaus Cty.) and we bought it for $11,000; it included eight cows and a small barn. We lived there for six years and then we bought the ten acres where this house is. My husband mortgaged the twenty acres which were clear then and joined a life insurance group to make sure that I wouldn't be left without anything if something should happen to him. Then we bought the twenty acres next to us and finally the next ten acres. I was unhappy when he bought the last ten acres because I thought we were never going to be out of debt. We finally ended up with sixty acres. It took us a long time to pay for it. It was just hard work and paying debts".[97]

Although whaling disappeared as an economic activity by the turn of the century, a relatively small number of Portuguese in California continued to earn their livelihood as commercial fishermen. The San Francisco Bay Area was the early center of Portuguese fishing, but in 1876 a small group of Azoreans, who had been working as fishermen in Gloucester, Massachusetts, decided to move to California. Part of the group went to the San Francisco area and the others ended up in the small city of San Diego where they settled on a point of land across the bay from the main part of town. Point Loma, as the area was named, gradually evolved into a self-sufficient Portuguese fishing community reminiscent of the Azores. The families raised their own fruit and vegetables, carried wood from the hills and beaches for cooking, and even brought fresh water in barrels from across the bay.[98] The Portuguese and Italians dominated the fresh fish business in

[97] Interview with Alexandrina Alves in Patterson, California, on Nov. 25, 1978.

[98] Oliver, *Never Backward*. Pp. 23—24.

San Diego; what was not sold locally was dried and sent north to the Central Valley. In the early part of the 20th century they began to pack the fish in ice and ship them to Los Angeles. As the fresh fish business prospered the immigrant fishermen maintained the tradition of encouraging relatives and friends to join them. The impetus for a major change in the Portuguese community of San Diego came out of World War I and the efforts to preserve fish by canning. In 1919 a Portuguese fisherman was hired to supply a local cannery with fresh tuna and the first attempt was made to preserve that particular variety of fish in a can.[99] Such was the beginning of the commercial tuna fishing fleet of San Diego and the Portuguese association with that industry. The San Diego tuna fleet grew rapidly after 1920 and was manned predominantly by Portuguese fishermen.[100] Although the number of Portuguese involved in the catching and canning of tuna remained small in relation to the total Portuguese population of California, they played a major role in the development of the tuna industry in San Diego. As the tuna fleet grew so did the close-knit Portuguese community on Point Loma and the association between the two was sufficiently strong that many of the people in San Diego came to refer to Point Loma as "Tunaville".[101] The tech ology employed in tuna fishing has changed radically since those early days in 1920, but the Portuguese have retained a prominent place in the industry.

Viewed collectively, the migration experience of a people frequently obscures the heartaches of dislocation, the fear of the unknown, the hardships and struggles involved in starting life anew, and the joys and sorrows that are a part of every day living for immigrants and non-immigrants alike. The most difficult aspect of a collective migration to capture and appreciate is the affect that the experience had on the individuals involved. The real life experience of a single individual related by a descendent, while not typical — in the sense that there is no such thing as a typical immigrant — illustrates the human side of the Azorean migration to California and the United States.

Manuel A. was born in the Azores on the island of Terceira in 1869 and was working as an errand boy when he decided to come to America to avoid being drafted into the Portuguese army. In 1889 some

[99] Frederick G. Williams, "Os Inicios da Pesca do Atum en San Diego". In *First Symposium on Portuguese Presence in California*. San Francisco, 1974. P. 7.

[100] H.C. Godsil, *The High Seas Tuna Fishery of California*. Sacramento, 1938. P. 17.

[101] Michael K. Orbach, *Hunters, Seamen and Entrepreneurs: The Tuna Seinermen of San Diego*. Berkeley, 1977. P. 7.

men hid him with the trunks in a cargo ship and he came to America as a stowaway on a sailing ship. It took him thirty-seven days to reach the United States. The first year he was in this country he worked in a lumber mill in Vermont for $20.00 a month, but it was awfully cold and he didn't like it. He decided to go to California where he had an older brother and ended up in San Francisco at the Portuguese Hotel. He stayed there until he got a job working in the lumber mills in Humboldt County at $25.00 a month. He saved his money and soon went into partnership with his brother in a small dairy where they separated the cream from the milk, sold the cream, and fed the skim milk to hogs. They raised their own vegetables, including potatoes, and butchered a hog when they needed meat; they only went to town twice a year to buy staples and supplies. The partnership lasted twelve years when they decided to sell out and Manuel returned to the Azores to see his mother.

When he was preparing to leave for the Azores, in 1905, a Portuguese woman in Arcadia asked him to take a few things back to her parents and sister who also lived in Terceira. He ended up marrying the woman's sister and they had four children in the Azores, but two of them — both girls — died of dysentery. After six years Dad realized that he could never be able to make a sufficient living in the Azores so he decided to return to America before he ran out of money. He left the Azores, for the second time, with his wife and two boys in 1911. This time the trip was made by steamship and took only seven days. One of the two boys got sick coming over and never fully recovered; he died after they reached California.

From the east coast the family traveled to California by train; it was a tiring, seven day trip across the country. Seven weary days of dirt from the soot and ashes of the train, and of caring for a sick boy. They returned to Arcadia where Mom's sister lived, but the area did not seem to offer much promise and after the boy died they moved to Gustine (Stanislaus County) where Dad's older brother had been since 1905 and Dad went back into partnership with him.

We lived in Gustine for three years and E. was born there in 1912. From there we moved to Turlock

(Stanislaus Cty.) where Dad bought a twenty-acre farm. We stayed there for three years and J. was born there in 1916. Afterwards we moved to Ceres (Stanislaus Cty.) where Dad operated a dairy on a share basis until 1925 when he bought a dairy in Salida (Stanislaus Cty.). Mom came down sick about a year after J. was born and had a major operation. Two years after we moved to Salida Mom died at the age of forty-nine. E. was fifteen then and had to take over the housekeeping duties; she had finished grammar school but she never went back to school.

In addition to the dairy, Dad raised melons, pumpkins, potatoes and vegetables of all kinds; what we didn't eat or give away was fed to the pigs. Times were difficult in the 1920s and 1930s. We raised most of our own food and we did without a lot of things. We received a new outfit of clothes once a year and the rest of the year the clothes were patched and repatched. There were few luxuries. E. took care of the house and M., the older brother, and J. helped on the dairy and worked part-time for the neighbors when they could.

In 1925 an epidemic of hoof-and-mouth disease broke out in the valley and all the infected cows had to be destroyed. It was especially bad in the Fresno, Merced and Gustine areas and everyone was under a great deal of pressure because they were afraid that it would hit their cows. Everyone was worried about the disease and when we went to school we had to dip our shoes in sheep dip — a disinfectant — when we arrived and when we left to go home. Some people had nervous breakdowns because they lost all their herd — it was a dreadful time. We didn't have any cows come down with it, but Dad was really worried. One day the dog followed our horses when a neighbor borrowed them and when the dog came back he was tired-out and had saliva dripping from his mouth. Dad was so afraid that the dog might have hoof-and-mouth disease and the dairy would end up quarantined and the cows killed that he killed our dog — the best dog we ever had. Dad was under a lot of tension.

We always spoke Portuguese at home. Dad could read and write English but Mom never learned any English. Mom never had the opportunity to go to school in the Azores, but Dad taught her how to sign her name. Dad received a Portuguese language newspaper from Oakland and used to read to Mom. When we lived in Ceres, the landlord used to teach us some English words, other than that we didn't know any English before we started to school.

The old timers thought it was more important for the children to help work at home than to go to school and get an education. You didn't need an education to farm; you needed to learn how to work and to farm. Dad kept M. out of school a lot to help with the work on the dairy and he didn't get much formal education. He also kept J. out of school to help. One day the truant officer came to our house and threatened to arrest Dad if he kept J. out of school one more time. The combination of trying to learn the language, moving several times, and missing a lot of school resulted in our repeating grades.

Dad never became a citizen — he was still afraid a war might break out and he would get called — that was the reason why he left the Azores. Mother never became a citizen either. Dad joined the UPEC (a fraternal organization for men) after he came back to California with his family and Mom belonged to the SPRSI (a fraternal organization for women). Both provided insurance benefits for their members. Dad sold the dairy cows in 1934 and leased the ranch. He died in 1942 at the age of 73.[102]

Between 1870 and 1900 two noticeable changes

---

[102] Interview with Elsie (Avila) Maciel and John Avila in Modesto, California, on November 24, 1978.

occurred in the Portuguese population of the United States: the first was a substantial increase in the absolute number of Portuguese, and the second was the sudden appearance of a significant Portuguese immigrant population in the Hawaiian Islands. The 8,605 foreign born Portuguese enumerated by the Census of 1870 had increased to 48,099 thirty years later. The relative distribution in 1900 closely followed the pattern which was well established by 1870. Massachusetts, California and Rhode Island accounted for 75.5 percent of the foreign born Portuguese, with an additional 15.9 percent of the American total located in Hawaii. These four political entities together represented 91.4 percent of all the foreign born Portuguese in the United States in 1900. By 1930, the number of foreign born Portuguese in the United States and its possessions exceeded 100,000 for the first time and when their American born offspring were included, the second generation, the total reached 278,726. The pattern of distribution, however, changed very little from 1900; Massachusetts, California, Rhode Island and Hawaii still accounted for 90.5 percent of all Portuguese foreign white stock. Hawaii and Rhode Island did switch relative ranks between 1900 and 1930; Rhode Island continued to attract Portuguese immigrants until the mid-1920s, but few Portuguese migrated to the Hawaiian Islands after 1900. Instead there was a noticeable out-migration of Portuguese immigrants from Hawaii to California. The relative concentration of Portuguese remained, however, within the same four political units (*See,* Table 1).

Proximity to the Azores was certainly not one of the attributes of the Hawaiian Islands; just getting there entailed a journey one-third of the way around the world. And yet, by 1900 sixteen percent of the foreign born Portuguese population of the United States and its territories were living in these islands. This sudden rise in the Portuguese population of the Hawaiian Islands is noteworthy both for the rapidity and the manner in which it occurred. Prior to 1870 there were only about 400 Portuguese living in the islands; virtually all of them were remnants, in one way or another, of the whaling era. From the 1840s, until whaling began its sharp decline in the 1870s, the Pacific whaling grounds were the major source of whales for the American fleet. During that time, and particularly after the discovery of gold in California, the Hawaiian Islands flourished as the principal outfitting and transshipment center for the Pacific whaling fleet. The large numbers of Azoreans engaged in whaling made it inevitable that many would come in contact with the Hawaiian Islands and that some would end up there permanently. Some deserted their ships, while others chose to remain in the islands when the whalers, laden with oil and bone, set sail for their home port in New England. The continuing shortage of crewmen made it easy to sign on

TABLE 1

PORTUGUESE POPULATION OF THE UNITED STATES: 1870—1930

Political Unit	1870		1900[1]		1930[2]		1930[a]	
	Number	%	Number	%	Number	%	Number	%
California	3,435	40.0	15,583	32.4	35,395	32.4	99.194	35.6
Connecticut	221	2.6	655	1.4	2,345	2.1	4.701	1.7
Hawaii	–	–	7,668	15.9	3,713	3.4	19.121	6.8
Illinois	856	9.9	–	–	–	–	–	–
Massachusetts	2,555	29.7	17,885	37.2	43,402	39.7	105.076	37.7
New Jersey	–	–	62	0.3	3,655	3.3	5.099	1.8
New York	334	3.9	823	1.7	7,758	7.1	7.758b	2.8
Rhode Island	189	2.2	2,865	5.9	11,679	10.7	29.097	10.4
All others	1,015	11.7	2,558	5.2	1,167	1.3	8.680	3.2
TOTAL	8,605	100.0	48,099	100.0	109,114	100.0	278.726	100.0

Source: [1]Twelfth Census of the United States, 1900, Vol. II, Population, Part II.

   [2]Fifteenth Census of the United States, 1930, Vol. III, Population, General Report.

Notes: [a] Foreign white stock. Includes foreign born Portuguese and their children – the first and second generation.

   [b] Data on foreign white stock of Portuguese heritage not listed for New York in 1930.

with another ship headed for the whaling grounds, and the islands, so similar to their homeland were, for many, preferable to the long journey back to the unfamiliar climate of New England. With the gradual decline of whaling, the Portuguese who remained in the islands reverted to a lifestyle more typical of their homeland.

With its rich volcanic soils and tropical climate, Hawaii possessed two of the three basic ingredients necessary to develop and sustain a substantial sugar cane industry. The only thing lacking was a continuous supply of cheap labor; to solve that problem the government, in conjunction with the plantation owners, turned to immigration from abroad. Chinese men were the first group to come to Hawaii to work in the cane fields in any substantial numbers; but the government was unsuccessful in its efforts to attract Chinese women to immigrate to the islands. The arrival of large numbers of single Chinese males soon aroused a negative reaction among the general population of the islands and the plantation owners and government began to cast about in search of a source of family immigrants as a long-term solution to the need for plantation workers. The former whalers from the Azores and Madeira Islands had, for the most part, turned to agriculture by the 1870s, either on their own small farms or as workers on the plantations and ranches on the islands, and had proven themselves to be industrious workers.[103]

A former resident of Hawaii, ever alert to the planters' need for cheap labor and the opportunity to benefit personally from that need, made a strong case for importing Portuguese immigrants to solve the labor problem in the islands. In a letter from the Madeira Islands in 1876, he wrote,

> In my opinion your islands could not possibly get a more desirable class of immigrants than the population of the Madeira and Azore Islands. Sober, honest, industrious and peaceable, they combine all the qualities of a good settler and with all this, they are inured to your climate. Their education and ideas of comfort and social requirements are just low enough to make them content with the lot of an isolated settler and its attendant privations, while on

[103] Ralph S. Kuykendall, *The Hawaiian Kingdom*, Vol. III, *1874—1893, The Kalakaua Dynasty.* Honolulu, 1967. Pp. 119—122.

the other hand their mental capabilities and habits of
work will ensure them a much higher status in the
next generation...[104]

The Portuguese, to all appearances, were ideal candidates for the cane fields
and serious negotiations were soon initiated. When the final agreements
were completed in 1877, the board of immigration for the Hawaiian Islands
had agreed to incur the cost of transportation for immigrants and their
families from the Madeira and Azores Islands and to provide them with jobs,
at $10.00 per month, lodging, rations and medical care. On their part, the
Portuguese immigrants were required to sign a contract agreeing to work on
the plantations for 36 months. Withdrawing from the contract, or failure to
comply with it after reaching Hawaii, obligated the immigrant to reimburse
the board for the cost of his passage.

The first Portuguese immigrants arrived in Honolulu
in 1878; between then and 1899, twenty-one ships deposited 12,780 Madeiran
and Azorean Islanders in Hawaii.[105] Eleven of the twenty-one were sailing
vessels and for them it was a long, slow trip from the eastern Atlantic Ocean,
around Cape Horn and on to the Hawaiian Islands. One of the 400 passengers
sailing on the ship *Thomas Bell* in 1887 kept a daily journal of the 156 day
trip; his remarkable account recreates in microcosm the experiences of many
of the Portuguese immigrants bound for Hawaii: rough seas, disease, deaths,
births, marriages, becalmed seas, food shortages, infestations of bedbugs,
stormy weather, fights between passengers and crew and among the
passengers themselves, boredom, promiscuity, the Christmas season, dancing,
fishing, and waiting — such was their lot.[106]

Of the 12,780 Portuguese immigrants who arrived
between 1878 and 1899, 42 percent were men, 19 percent women, and 39
percent children. The Census of 1900, taken just two years after Hawaii was
annexed to the United States in July, 1898, recorded 7,668 foreign born
Portuguese in the islands; [107] most of them were relatively new arrivals.

---

[104] *Ibid.* P. 123.

[105] Lucile de Silva Canario (trans.), "Destination, Sandwich Islands, Nov. 8, 1887". By Joao
Baptista d'Oliveira and Vincente d'Ornellas. In *The Hawaiian Journal of History,* Vol. 4, 1970.
Pp. 49—51.

[106] *Ibid.* Pp. 3—50.

[107] *Twelfth Census of the United States, 1900,* Vol. 2, *Population,* Part 2. Washington, D.C.,
1900.

Between 1906 and 1909 three more steamships arrived with an additional 3,314 immigrants, thereby raising the total number of Portuguese who immigrated as contract laborers to 16,094.[108] The apparent success in attracting Portuguese families to immigrate to Hawaii was tempered by the expense of the program; the long voyage from the Madeira and Azores Islands together with the high percentage of children resulted in a high cost per working immigrant. After complying with the terms of their contract, many of the early immigrants took advantage of their relative proximity to the west coast of the continental United States and moved on to California. Some of the later arrivals left almost immediately for California.[109] The planters and government soon came to the conclusion that the liabilities of sponsoring Portuguese immigration were greater than the benefits and began to seek a supply of cheap labor closer to home. Their subsequent success in attracting cane field workers from Japan brought a close to the importation of Portuguese as contract laborers to Hawaii.

Portuguese immigrants in Hawaii found themselves in a somewhat different position, *vis-à-vis* the dominant social group, than did their counterparts in Massachusetts and Rhode Island. On the east coast of the continental United States, the Portuguese were just one of a myriad of ethnic groups pouring into the country. And if they were poor, spoke a foreign language, and had different customs, they were generically indistinguishable from millions of other immigrants who were also poor, spoke a foreign language, and adhered to different customs. Although the Portuguese who entered the Hawaiian Islands after 1878 were grudgingly acknowledged, as southern Europeans, to be caucasians in a caucasian dominated society, they were in the unfortunate position of having arrived in large numbers, possessing few worldly goods, and, as contract labor, occupying the absolute bottom of the economic ladder. They quickly came to be looked down upon as "an inferior people of low economic and social status.[110] The connotation of farm laborer or independent agriculturalist was quite different in the diversified economy of the continental United States than it was in the plantation economy of Hawaii where agricultural workers were at the very bottom of the social system. The negative association of agriculture and

---

[108] Canario, "Destination, Sandwich Islands". Pp. 51–52.

[109] Nancy F. Young (compiler), *The Portuguese in Hawaii: A Resource Guide*. Honolulu, 1973. P. 11.

[110] Gerald Allan Estep, "Social Placement of the Portuguese in Hawaii as Indicated by Factors in Assimilation". Unpublished M.A. Thesis, University of Southern California, 1941. P. 16.

social status quickly became apparent to the Portuguese immigrants and they reacted in a variety of ways, almost all of which served to put as much distance as possible, either physical or social, between themselves and other contract laborers. Many completely removed themselves from the islands by migrating to the mainland; between 1911 and 1914, for example, over two thousand relocated in California.[111] Others "worked their way urbanward as fast as possible to escape the stigma attached to lowly plantation labor and to better their economic conditions...".[112]

In marked contrast to the Portuguese on the east coast of the United States, who collectively reinforced their cultural heritage and maintained their ethnic identity, Portuguese immigrants in Hawaii

> disbanded as a nationality group, settled apart from one another and preferably, in *haole*-occupied areas. They associated with other than their own group, modifying old-world customs and taking on new ones, marrying outside the group and especially into the haole group, giving up old-world institutions and languages, even changing their names in some instances. Anything and everything justified in order to obliterate the haole stereotype of a "Portagee".[113]

Initially brought in as laborers for the sugar cane plantations, their early settlement pattern coincided with the sugar producing islands. By 1900, however, the total Portuguese foreign born population had declined to 7,668 and was concentrated primarily on the island of Oahu, Honolulu County, which had 38.1 percent of the total, and the big island of Hawaii, with 35.6 percent (*See,* Map 6). Unlike the mainland, where new immigrants continued to arrive until they were slowed down by the literacy requirement of 1917 and then shut out by the National Origin's legislation of the 1920s, after the Hawaiian Islands discontinued sponsoring contract labor from the Madeira and Azores Islands in the first decade of the 20th century, the flow of Portuguese immigration ceased. And, as previously noted, a reverse flow of Portuguese out-migration from the Hawaiian Islands

---

[111] Gerald Allen Estep, "Portuguese Assimilation in Hawaii and California", *Sociology and Social Research,* Vol. 26, Sept.—Oct., 1941. P. 61.

[112] *Ibid.* P. 62.

[113] *Ibid.* P. 67.

MAP 6

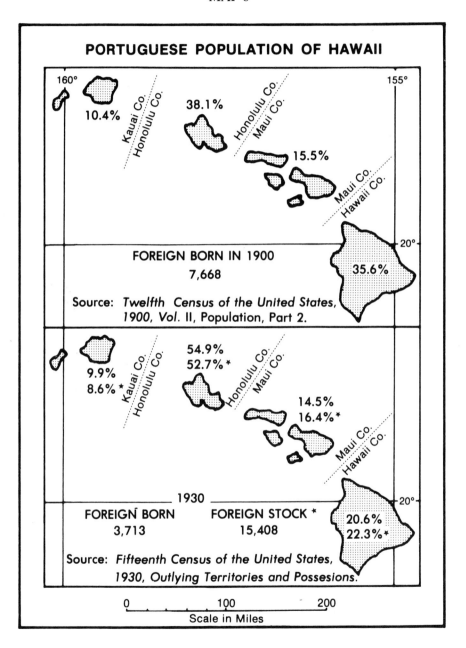

PORTUGUESE POPULATION OF HAWAII

160°

Kauai Co.
Honolulu Co.

10.4%

38.1%

Honolulu Co.
Maui Co.

15.5%

Maui Co.
Hawaii Co.

155°

20°

FOREIGN BORN IN 1900
7,668

35.6%

Source: *Twelfth Census of the United States, 1900, Vol. II, Population, Part 2.*

Kauai Co.
Honolulu Co.

9.9%
8.6%*

54.9%
52.7%*

Honolulu Co.
Maui Co.

14.5%
16.4%*

Maui Co.
Hawaii Co.

1930

FOREIGN BORN   FOREIGN STOCK *
3,713   15,408

20.6%
22.3%*

20°

Source: *Fifteenth Census of the United States, 1930, Outlying Territories and Possesions.*

0   100   200

Scale in Miles

to the mainland replaced the earlier immigration. Instead of encouraging friends and relatives to join them in the Hawaiian Islands, the immigrants utilized their social network to advise other potential immigrants to go elsewhere and, in fact, to make contact on the mainland so they themselves could leave the islands.

According to the Census of 1930, there were 15,048 individuals classified as Portuguese foreign stock living in the Hawaiian Islands. Only 3,713 of those, however, were foreign born. The relocation within the islands, first noticeable in 1900, became even more accentuated by 1930 when over 50 percent of both the Portuguese foreign born and foreign stock were concentrated in Honolulu County on the island of Oahu. The most obvious decline in the percentage of Portuguese living in the islands were registered by the island of Hawaii which went from 35.6 percent of the foreign born in 1900 to 20.6 percent in 1930 (*See,* Map 6). Although the total foreign born Portuguese population of the Hawaiian Islands declined after 1900, the size of the original immigrant population imported into the islands as contract laborers, together with their offspring, was sufficiently large to maintain Hawaii's position as one of the major concentrations of Portuguese in the United States and its territories through the mid-1900s.

Chapter IV

Emigration: A Response
to Adversity and Opportunity

Behind the precipitous cliff coasts, common throughout the Azores, are silent reminders of the volcanic activity which created these islands; enormous calderas; craters of extinct and dormant volcanoes; areas of bubbling mud pots and thermal springs; ancient lava flows weathered by vegetation and climate; the still unweathered scars of historically recent lava flows; and, the 7,615-foot towering volcano which constitutes virtually all of the island of Pico and serves as the landmark for the archipelago. Tree covered hills, rock strewn fields and a scarcity of flat land are combined with a humid but mild climate to create a picturesque setting for the visitor, but an environment which necessitates diligence and hard work on the part of the inhabitants.

In their natural state, when they were first discovered by the Portuguese in the early 15th century, these islands provided a sufficient resource base for a modest agrarian population. Although the amount of level land was limited, the soil was rich; precipitation was adequate — from about 50 inches annually on Flores to about 35 inches per year on Santa Maria; and the slopes were covered with forest. Lacking any other raw materials, the early inhabitants were forced to rely upon the soil and they quickly developed a sy. em of agriculture adapted to their environment. To clear the rock strewn fields, they built stone walls which also served to mark property lines; the forested slopes provided charcoal for fuel, and the cleared land was ideal for pasture. Lacking good harbors, they relied on small boats to fish the surrounding waters to supplement their diet. In short, the early settlers developed a survival technique well suited to their particular environment.

Few people, however, are satisfied with just surviving; particularly those who underwrote the expense of sending colonists to develop and exploit land given to them by the crown of Portugal. The elusive search for a rewarding cash crop suitable to these islands began with the first settlers in the fifteenth century and is still being sought today. In many ways, the economic history of the Azores is reminiscent of that of Brazil which was also settled by the Portuguese. In both cases, the inhabitants came to depend upon a particular crop or product which dominated the economy only to see it eventually collapse, due to competition from abroad or a decline in productivity, and be slowly replaced by another product which repeated the cycle. By developing its enormous deposits of mineral wealth, Brazil finally escaped the repetitious cycles of a "boom and bust" economy in the 20th century; but, in the Azores, the search continues. In the process, plants and animals have been imported from all over the world. Some proved beneficial; others were disastrous, but each had an impact on the islands.

One of the first cash crops to be introduced was sugar cane, but it quickly gave way to the woad plant — an important source of blue dye in the fifteenth and sixteenth century. By the mid-seventeenth century, indigo from America captured the world dye market and displaced woad. Wheat and flax were temporary substitutes, but wheat is an extensive crop requiring large areas to produce in any quantity and flax was most valuable for export after it had been processed into linens. Neither provided a satisfactory cash crop ideally suited to the environments found in these islands. Citrus and wine grapes were both important in the mid-18th century. England was the destination of most of the fruit grown in the Azores; from 1747 until 1838 lemons were one of the major products. In 1838, England found a better supply of lemons elsewhere and the market collapsed. By this time, however, oranges had also become a very important export crop. In 1802 nearly 40,000 boxes of oranges were shipped to London alone and by the 1870s some 500,000 boxes, each containing from 300-400 oranges, was annually sent to the English market from São Miguel alone.[114]

Hardy plants by nature, grapevines were a logical choice for planting in rocky soils unsuitable for cultivation or pastures. But, the successful cultivation of wine grapes in the islands required a considerable input of ingenuity and hard work. For the grapes to mature with a sufficient sugar content to make good wine, the vineyards needed to be protected from

---

[114] Walter Walker, *The Azores or Western Islands: A Political, Commercial and Geographical Account* (London, 1886), p. 86.

the strong winds characteristic of the Azores. Removing the surface stones from even the rockiest areas usually uncovered sufficient soil to plant the vines; these stones were then converted into walls to provide a windbreak. Row after row of small, irregular shaped cubicles, often encasing no more than one hundred square feet with stone walls three to four feet high, gradually spread over the rocky lowlands. Viewed from the nearby hills, these vineyards created a very distinctive pattern on the land — not unlike a labryinthian maze spreading over the hills. Once the technique was perfected, it spread throughout the islands and wine became an increasingly important cash crop. By 1850, the island vineyards were annually producing 50,000 pipes of very good wine.[115]

In the continuing search for new cash crops, pineapples were introduced in the 1860s and by the mid-1880s more than 125,000 pineapples a year were being exported to England. However, pineapples in the Azores are a capital intensive crop that require hot houses and intensive care to produce. Intially introduced into the Ponta Delgada area of São Miguel, they never spread to other areas and are still grown there today. In 1878 tea was introduced as a new commerical crop.[116] Ideally suited for growing on the hilly uplands, enough tea is still produced on São Miguel to satisfy the islands' needs and for exporting to mainland Portugal, but tea grown here could not compete with tea grown in the Far East and another plan fizzled.

Every new crop introduced to the islands, with the expectation that it would prove to be a valuable cash crop and an asset to the local economy, had a particular impact on the local environment. Some, such as potatoes, beans and corn became the mainstay of the population and spread throughout the islands. Others, such as tobacco, depleted the soil and used up some of the best land. Still others necessitated the clearing and cultivation of additional land, or like oranges, made their demands upon the environment in a different form. Shipping hundreds of thousands of boxes of oranges from the Azores to England in the period from 1800 to 1880 required substantial quantities of wood for fruit boxes. The gradual deforestation of the islands in search of box wood quickened in times of crises when alternate supplies were restricted or cut off; by the late 1830s desperate orange

---

[115] *Ibid.,* P. 91. A pipe was a unit of measure equivalent to two hogsheads — each of which contained 63 gallons. Each pipe of wine then was approximately 125 gallons.

[116] *Ibid.,* Pp. 91-96.

exporters were "forced to cut down every available tree they could procure".[117] After most of the useable timber was removed from the islands to make fruit boxes, fast growing trees were introduced from various parts of the world to try to satisfy the demand for wood. Among the trees introduced for this purpose were: the Japanese cedar, *Cryptomeria japonica;* Eucalyptus from Australia; the acasia tree, *Acasia melanoxylon;* and several varieties of pine, including *Pinus maritima. Pittosporum* was introduced from Australia in the 1840s to serve as a windbreak for oranges, thereby enabling citrus orchards to expand into less favorable parts of the islands. Only after the pittosporum spread did the orchardists realize that it also exhausted the soil.[118]

The Azores have a very limited amount of land and the use of that land is restricted by both elevation and relief. In general, agriculture is limited to the relatively flat areas below 1,000 feet with pasture, forest and rough land occupying the rest. Settlements and roads, virtually all along the coast, and other uses compete with agriculture for the useable lowlands (*See,* Table 2).

When the New England whalers began stopping in the Azores for fresh supplies at the beginning of the nineteenth century, the islands were no longer in their natural state. Small villages dotted the coastline and the land suitable for agriculture had already been intensively farmed for over 300 years. Livestock grazed on the slopes which were once heavily wooded but had long since been exploited for fuel and useable timber. A general system of specialization, based upon the characteristics of each island, had gradually evolved in the archipelago. São Miguel, the only island with a substantial amount of good agricultural land, was always in the forefront of the search for a remunerative cash crop. Almost all of the commercial crops were introduced to that island first and most were never even marginally successful elsewhere, including: tobacco, tea, pineapples, and sugar cane. São Miguel was also the major producer of citrus fruit in the 18th and 19th centuries. Like all of the islands, a major portion of the agricultural land was devoted to subsistence crops to feed the local population. Neither Terceira nor São Jorge possessed much good agricultural land, but both were well suited to raising cattle and became noted early for their cattle and dairy products. Faial and Pico, the two geographically closest islands —

[117] *Ibid.,* P. 101.

[118] *Ibid.,* Pp. 91-99

TABLE 2
AREA AND GENERAL ELEVATION OF
THE AZORES ISLANDS

Island	Area in Sq. Miles	% Below 1,000 Feet	% Above 1,000 Feet
Santa Maria	37	86.4	13.6
São Miguel	288	52.7	47.3
Terceira	153	55.6	44.4
Graciosa	24	94.5	5.7
São Jorge	92	30.1	69.9
Pico	168	41.2	58.8
Faial	66	53.5	46.5
Flores	55	32.5	67.5
Corvo	6.7	45.1	54.9
TOTAL	889.7		

Source: *Acores: do 25 de Abril até aos nossos dias,* p. 150.

yet physically dissimilar—developed a complementary system of agriculture. Diversified farming, including the cultivation of fruits, vegetables and grains was common on Faial. Pico, the second largest island, has very little land suited for general agriculture. Much of the rocky lowlands were converted to vineyards and livestock were raised on the uplands. The variety of foodstuffs available from these two islands, in conjunction with an excellent harbor, soon made Horta, Faial the main Azorean port of call for the whaling vessels. Graciosa and, to a lesser degree, Santa Maria developed vineyards to complement their livelihood — subsistence agriculture. Flores and Corvo, the two smallest and most isolated islands, enjoyed even less favorable circumstances than the other seven islands and their populations have always been preoccupied with subsistence agriculture.[119]

[119] Graves, "Immigrants in Agriculture," Pp. 34-38.

In addition to their farming techniques, the early Portuguese settlers brought with them a system of land tenure which, in effect, relegated the masses to a permanent status as landless peasants. Under this system, known as the perpetual leasehold, the tenant farmer paid his rent either in kind, when the crop was harvested, or in cash at the end of the year. The amount of rent was fixed, however, and not alterable.[120] Unlike sharecropping, where the landowner and tenant share in both the good years and the bad, in this system of land tenure the risks were all assumed by the tenant. An unusually good harvest benefitted the peasants, but a crop failure could be devastating. Even worse, though, was the difficulty encountered by each peasant's offspring in finding land to farm. In 1840, the agricultural land in the islands was controlled by less than three percent of the total population.[121] The leases which most of the peasants had on the land were hereditary but they could not be sub-divided without the consent of the owner.[122] The number of peasants who not only did not own land, but could not even find land to farm, increased with each generation.

Nineteenth century life in the Azores was the product of over three hundred years of struggling to make a living from the soil in an isolated environment. A rigid social structure pervaded the lifestyle of the villages and exacerbated the lack of economic opportunity and upward mobility. Like most agrarian societies, the daily routine of life seldom changed and, in fact, was passed on from generation to generation. Children were born, raised, and eventually died in the village of their birth and, while an individual's virtues were well known throughout the village, so were his vices. Even so, the individual knew exactly who he was and where he fit into the social and economic life of his island. He might not like his position in life or his general inability to change it, but there was no such thing as an identity crisis. In times of stress, the extended family, aided by an intricate and reciprocal system of god-parentage, could always be relied upon for assistance. Living in the same village generation after generation eventually resulted in an extended family system whereby virtually everyone in the village was related in one way or another. Within this close-knit society, the individual identified most clearly with his particular village and the island on which it was located. Little, if any, thought was given to the fact that these islands, collectively known as the Azores, were considered by the Portuguese crown

---

[120] Walker, *The Azores or Western Islands,* Pp. 78-79.

[121] Graves, "Immigrants in Agriculture," P. 34.

[122] Walker, *The Azores or Western Islands,* P. 79.

to be an integral part of Portugal or that the inhabitants were Portuguese citizens.

Compulsory military service for all young males was a persistent and unpopular burden of Portuguese citizenship for the Azoreans. At the age of sixteen, every male faced the prospects of eight years of military service in mainland Portugal.[123] This obligation weighed particularly heavy upon the peasant class. Although it was common practice to hire a substitute to serve the military duty, in reality this was an option only available to families with sufficient wealth to hire a substitute. As one observer noted in the 1880s, "The Azorean islander flies from the recruiting sergeant as he would from the Evil One, and, to escape service will run any risks ..."[124] One of the options to military service which presented itself in the 19th century was to ship out as a common sailor on an American whaling vessel. Many young Azoreans peasants, with no sailing experience, took advantage of the option. Since it was illegal for young men to leave the islands without making a monetary payment to hire a substitute for military service, most of these departures were of a clandestine nature.

Like all agrarian societies, the Azoreans were dependent upon the soil for their survival and although there were occasional crop failures, as there are in any agricultural society, the surpluses and shortages tended to balance out. By the 19th century, however, these nine islands, which were clearly capable of providing a satisfactory life for a modest number of people, were seriously overpopulated. The normal vicissitudes of an agrarian economy became fraught with anxiety as hunger more frequently accompanied crop failure. As one observer recorded,

> when there is a scarcity, which is the case sometimes, it is not because the islands are unproductive, but because they are overloaded with population, and the crops are injured by incessant rains or strong winds. [125]

Although the first official Census of Portugal was not taken until 1864, the problem of too many people and too little land was apparent long before then (*See,* Table 3).

What everyone living in the islands already knew, the Census of 1864 made official; the pressure on the limited amount of

---

[123] Berger, *In Great Waters,* Pp. 45-46.

[124] Walker, *The Azores or Western Islands,* Pp. 111-112.

[125] Borges de F. Henriques, *A Trip to the Azores or Western Islands* (Boston, 1867), P. 30.

TABLE 3

AREA, POPULATION AND DENSITY OF THE
AZORES ISLANDS, 1865

Islands	Area in Sq. Miles	Population	Persons per Sq. Mile
Santa Maria	37	5,863	158
São Miguel	288	105,404	366
Terceira	153	45,781	300
Graciosa	24	8,718	366
São Jorge	92	17,998	195
Pico	168	27,721	165
Faial	66	26,259	398
Flores	55	10,259	191
Corvo	6.7	883	131
TOTAL	889.7	249,135	280

Source: *Sumula de Dados Estatisticos, Departmento Regional de Estudos e Planeamento, Acores,* 1976, p.4.

agricultural land had become intense. Although the official population density ranged from a high of 398 persons per square mile on Faial to a low of 131 on Corvo, the real density was much higher. Population densities are calculated by dividing the total population by the total land area and, in the Azores, much of that land was unusable. With less than forty percent of the surface area of these islands suitable for agriculture, the average population density for this land was closer to seven hundred persons per square mile in 1864.[126] TheAzorean peasant became adept at intensive agriculture on a very small scale. Yet, even good farmers occasionally get poor yields, and there is an absolute limit to the number of people a subsistence economy can sustain. Attempts to increase production occasionally backfired with serious results. In 1835, an American brought in a new variety of orange tree from Florida

[126] *Sumula de Dados Estatisticos* (Acores, 1976), P. 2.

which was, unbeknownst to him, infected with the orange parasite *Aspidiota conchiformis*. The parasite gradually spread throughout the islands and started the decline in commercial orange production.[127] Few alternatives to farming existed in the islands. The New England whalers offered an escape from the hand-to-mouth existence of subsistence farming and the obligation to serve in the Portuguese military. The occasional departee of the 1800s was replaced by a steady trickle of men in the 1820s and a flowing stream of escapees by 1840.

The arrival of two unwanted visitors to the Azores Islands in the early 1850s caused great consternation and hastened the departure of many young men to the California gold fields. The first of these was a potato rot that struck at the very heart of the islanders' diet. It was followed, in 1835, by a deadly fungus, *Oidium tuckeri*, which struck the grape vines in the islands and rapidly spread, with disastrous results, throughout the archipelago.[128] Wine production declined precipitously; "proprietors who used to have one thousand barrels of wine yearly, have now, some seasons, scarcely thirty".[129] Potatoes, the principal subsistence crop, were grown on all the islands and the effects of the potato rot were widely felt. Wine production, though found on almost all the islands, was heavily concentrated on Pico and to a lesser extent on Graciosa. The loss of their vineyards struck particularly hard at the inhabitants of Pico. Seriously deficient in agricultural land, they were unable to switch to other crops to replace the vines. With few alternatives readily available, the men of Pico turned to whaling — almost with a vengeance.

Pico's proximity to and association with Faial gave these islanders ample opportunity to join the whaleships calling at Horta Faial. An initial attempt to introduce shore whaling to the island of Faial in 1832 was unsuccessful, but conditions had changed by the early 1850s and the second effort succeeded. Shore whaling for sperm whales, employing the same techniques that were used along the New England coast in the 17th century, gradually spread to the other islands, but Pico and Faial dominated whaling in the Azores.[130] The men of Pico acquired the reputation of fearless whalers, both in the islands and on board the New England whaleships, and

[127] Walker, *The Azores or Western Islands*, P. 86.

[128] *Ibid.*, P. 91.

[129] Henriques, *A Trip to the Azores*, Pp. 31-32.

[130] Clarke, "Open Boat Whaling in the Azores,". P. 352.

that reputation is still widely known and maintained in the islands today. Shore whaling never provided an adequate livelihood for a substantial number of Azoreans however, and throughout the islands men were forced to turn elsewhere to earn a living. The flow of immigrants to America continued to increase.

In the fifty years between 1870 and 1920, the "pull" of America became irresistible for millions of Europeans. America was a new beginning for people who, for one reason or another, had never really had a first chance. Government land was free to anyone who was willing to go to the frontier, stake out a homestead and work to improve it. Granted, the land was on the fringes of civilization, sometimes of marginal value for cultivation, often with little or no water, and frequently lacking in trees, but it was free. For the non-farmers, the steam-powered industrial revolution sweeping the United States in the post-Civil War period required labor and still more labor. Often the hours were long, the working conditions poor and the wages minimal, but there were jobs. In spite of the many problems encountered: problems of language, of housing, and of discrimination — the United States still offered a chance for a better life, and immigrants responded in ever-increasing numbers. The attraction of America as the land of opportunity was further enhanced by conditions in Europe. Agrarian difficulties became widespread on the continent in the 1880s and everywhere population growth was pressuring available resources; at a time when surplus population was being forced from the land, viable alternatives were few and far between. As the *pogroms* in Western Russia in the 1880s demonstrated, the political climate was such, in many countries, that identifiable minority groups were being pushed from their homeland and forced to seek refuge elsewhere. The increasing awareness of opportunities in the New World together with improvements in land transportation on the continent and sea transportation across the Atlantic, made Europeans both aware of alternatives and willing to pursue them. Tens of millions of immigrants responded by abandoning their homelands for a new life in the United States, Canada, or South America.[131]

Isolated though they were from the mainstream of European life, even the Azores Islands could not escape the changes besetting the world at the end of the 19th century. Adversity, an infrequent visitor to these islands prior to 1850, became a constant companion after the 1870s.

---

[131] Philip Taylor, *The Distant Magnet: European Emigration to the U.S.A.* (N. Y., 1971), Pp.1-65.

The orange blight, which was accidentally introduced into the islands in 1835, gradually spread from island to island and appeared in São Miguel, the center of orange production, in 1877. By the mid-1880s, the citrus crop had declined to less than one-third of what it had been in 1870.[132] The grape fungus, which caused such precipitous declines in wine production when it first infested the islands' vineyards in 1853, established such a pervasive grip on the crop that it was not brought under control until the mid-20th century when new methods of combatting it were introduced.[133] Accompanying the devastating drop in commercial production was a comparable decline in subsistence crops. In an account of the islands published in 1886, it was noted:

> In 1876-77 there commenced that general failure of crops, which has recurred every year with more or less intensity to the present time, causing a complete stagnation in trade, and reducing numbers of families dependent upon the produce of their lands to considerable straits.[134]

The people of the Azores responded to their misfortunes as best they could; like people everywhere in times of trouble, they worked harder, to little or no avail, borrowed money from their more fortunate relatives and friends and, when all else failed, began to consider the alternative of leaving — of migrating to a new country. Still relatively minor in 1870, emigration continued to increase as conditions deteriorated during the last three decades of the 19th century and the population of the islands slowly but steadily mounted. Although the data necessary to calculate the actual rate of population growth for this period is nonexistent, the Census of 1911 provided some insights into what was happening demographically. Based on the crude birth and death rates reported in that census, an average annual natural increase of 11.99 per 1,000 population, 1.19 percent per annum, was arrived at for the archipelago.[135]

Within the Azores there was considerable variation in the growth rate: Horta District, comprised of the islands of Pico, Faial, Flores and Corvo, had a natural increase of 5.5 per thousand (0.55 percent);

---

[132] Walker, *The Azores or Western Islands,* Pp. 88-91.

[133] Clarke, "Open Boat Whaling in the Azores," P. 77.

[134] Walker, *The Azores or Western Islands,* P. 77.

[135] Taft, *Two Portuguese Communities in New England,* P. 53.

in the Angra District, the islands of Terceira, São Jorge and Graciosa, the rate was 6.65 (0.66 percent); while in the Ponta Delgada District, São Miguel and Santa Maria, where almost half of the total population resided, the annual natural increase was 12.58 per thousand (1.25 percent).[136] Even though it is impossible to determine precisely what the rate of increase was for the period between 1864 and the Census of 1904, it is possible to estimate a general range within which the population growth of these islands most probably fell. If, in the forty years preceding the 1904 Census, the islands had experienced an average annual natural increase of 1.0 percent, and there had been no emigration, the total population of the islands in 1904 would have been aproximately 350,000 persons. Conversely, if the average annual natural increase for the forty-year period had been only 0.5 percent, again with no emigration, the population in 1904 would have been slightly in excess of 300,000 individuals. Although the former is probably high and latter possibly low, neither is outside the range of population growth which was occurring throughout Europe at that time.[137] A comparison of the Census of 1864 with that of 1904 and 1920 illuminates, somewhat, the issues of both population growth within the islands and emigration from them (*See,* Table 4).

The apparent change in population between 1864 and 1904 is based on the enumerated population living in the islands at the later date and does not reflect the actual number of people who emigrated because it does not include the natural increase in population which also occurred over those forty years. By looking at the six islands that had an obvious decline in population, Graciosa, São Jorge, Pico, Faial, Flores and Corvo, it appears that they lost a total of 19,000 inhabitants — some 22 percent of their 1864 population. In reality, however, the actual number of emigrants was equal to the apparent 19,000 loss plus the total natural increase in their combined populations. What the natural increase in the population of that portion of the Azores was during those forty years is not certain; the best estimate is that it was somewhere between 20,000 and 42,000 people. What is certain, is that by 1920 when the out-migration began to diminish as a result of restrictive legislation in the United States, the total loss through migration had resulted in a substantial reduction in the population density of those six islands. Faial went from 398 persons per square mile in 1864 to 286 in 1920, representing an average reduction of 112 persons per square mile! Flores' population density dropped almost 70 per square mile,

[136] *Ibid.*

[137] Taylor, *The Distant Magnet,* Pp. 1-65.

TABLE 4

POPULATION OF THE AZORES ISLANDS 1864—1920

Islands	1864	1904	Apparent Change Since 1864 %	1920	Apparent Change Since 1904 %	Persons Per Sq. Mile 1920
Santa Maria	5,863	6,479	+10.5	6,457	- 0.3	174
São Miguel	105,404	120,354	+14.2	111,745	- 7.2	388
Terceira	45,781	48,098	+ 5.1	46,277	- 3.8	302
São Jorge	17,998	14,390	-20.0	13,362	- 7.1	145
Pico	27,721	22,926	-17.3	19,925	-13.1	118
Faial	26,259	19,075	-27.4	18,917	- 0.8	286
Flores	10,259	7,527	-26.6	6,720	-10.7	122
Corvo	888	758	-14.2	661	-12.8	98
TOTAL	249,135	247,686	- 0.6	231,543	- 6.5	260

Source: *Populacão dos Acores. Departmento Regional de Estudios e Planeamento, Acores, 1975, p. 1.*

while Pico, Graciosa and São Jorge each declined by approximately 50 people per square mile in the same period.

Even though Santa Maria, São Miguel and Terceira together ended up with 17,883 more inhabitants in 1904 than in 1864, 11.4 percent more, the increase was substantially lower than would be expected through natural increase. If the annual rate of natural increase had been 0.5 percent, and there had been no emigration, the combined population of the three islands would have approached 190,000; with 1.0 percent annual rate, and no emigration, their population would have exceeded 230,000 in 1904. In spite of their overall increase in population by 1904, a substantial out-migration did take place from Santa Maria, São Miguel and Terceira during these forty years. Between 1904 and 1920 emigration increased rapidly and the population of the three islands declined by 10,452 people, an apparent 6 percent drop in population. Again, if the natural increase is taken into account, which was determined to be 1.2 percent annually on Santa Maria and São Miguel in 1911, the number of people who left during the sixteen years was at least double and probably triple the indicated apparent decline. However large the out-migration was from these islands, it was not sufficient to compensate for the natural increase in population. In 1920, the population density on São Miguel reached 388 persons per square mile — an increase of 22 people per square mile in the 56 years. On Santa Maria, the increase averaged 16 per square mile during that same period. Terceira, somewhat more fortunate, lost virtually as many emigrants as it gained new population and was thereby almost able to maintain the *status quo*. In spite of the heavy out-migration that had taken place, what had been a difficult situation in 1864, with half of the population of the Azores crowded on these three islands, had, in fact, worsened by 1920.

The government of Portugal, seemingly oblivious to conditions on the islands and, no doubt, preoccupied with events elsewhere, did not make the decision to emigrate any easier. Cognizant of the ever increasing number of emigrants who were trying to escape an apparently hopeless existence and ever watchful to ensure a continuous supply of military conscripts, the Portuguese government passed a law in April, 1873, whereby "monetary payment in substitution of enlistment was abolished, and the unhappy emigrate was still liable to be called upon to serve, if he returned prior to attaining his 36th year":[138] It soon became apparent to the government that without being permitted to provide a substitute for military

---

[138] Walker, *The Azores or Western Islands*, P. 112.

service, young men would surreptitiously leave the country and not return — thereby inflicting a double loss to the country: the disappearance of a worker whose product might be taxed and the absence of a potential military conscript. The government quickly moved to rectify its error and in 1880, the Cortes passed a law compelling all males, when they reached the age of 14, to deposit £40 with the State before they would be permitted to leave the country. The £40 was to be kept in pawn; should the emigrant not return to serve his military duty, the money would be used to hire a substitute.[139] Laws have always been easier to enact than they are to enforce and this one was no exception. In 1886, it was noted that "Emigration, generally clandestine, has of late years greatly relieved the necessitous condition of these poor islanders" even though "the difficulties in the way of the over-plus population seeking their fortune elsewhere have been increased".[140] After years of thwarting the law, the alternatives sometime become as institutionalized as the laws themselves. When, in 1903, a boy from Pico finally persuaded his father to let him emigrate to America, to join his sister in New Bedford, clandestine departures were still common practice.

> Because of my age, fifteen, the government would not give me a passport. The government wanted the boys to wait until they were eighteen, then go to serve in the army for two or three years. My father had to pay an agent to smuggle me out of the Azores. The agents were professional smugglers. They operated regular services, for which young men paid a fee in order to get out of the islands.[141]

No fewer than twenty-two other young men were smuggled out in the same boat and although there was always the chance that these illegal emigrants would be apprehended by a Portuguese revenue cutter and returned to face a heavy fine, the likelihood of such an event occurring was more in the realm of a slim possibility than a real probability.

The Azores were not alone with their problems of declining agricultural productivity and increasing population; similar conditions existed in mainland Portugal and the Madeira Islands and the inhabitants responded in the same way — they sought new opportunities

---

[139] *Ibid.,* P. 107.

[140] *Ibid.*

[141] Oliver, *Never Backward,* P. 10.

elsewhere. Portuguese citizens were fortunate, in one way, during the 19th
and 20th century, in that several options were open to them. They could
migrate elsewhere within the Portuguese Empire, such as to Mozambique or
to Angola in Africa, or to Brazil, a former part of the Empire that became an
independent South American republic in 1888. Moving to a Portuguese
speaking country with similar customs made the transition easier than going
to a completely foreign country such as the United States.

Prior to about 1900, official records of the number of
emigrants leaving Portugal, including the Azores, are virtually nonexistent;
after 1900 the records are incomplete with entire years unaccounted for or
only partially recorded. What records do exist are for legal departures only
and do not include the unofficial emigrants who, by all accounts, comprised a
substantial number from the Azores Islands. Between 1890 and 1921,
official records indicate that of the approximately one million Portuguese
who emigrated from their homeland only 16 percent were destined for
America. The vast majority of emigrants were from the mainland and their
destination was overwhelmingly (85 percent) to Brazil. Only about 5 percent
of the mainland Portuguese (Continentals) ended up in the United States; the
others went to Europe and Africa. Of the recorded emigration from the
Azores, 82 percent chose to go to the United States, 16 percent selected
Brazil and the balance was lightly scattered between Europe and Africa.
Within the islands, there was considerable variation from district to district:
in Horta District, Pico, Faial, Flores, and Corvo, 94 percent emigrated to the
United States and 5 percent went to Brazil; in Ponta Delgada District, São
Miguel and Santa Maria, 84 percent selected the United States and 14
percent chose Brazil; in Angra District, Terceira, São Jorge, and Graciosa,
the percentages were 68 and 31 respectively. The Madeira Islands, with a
much smaller emigrant population during these years, were primarily oriented
to Brazil, where more than half of their out-migration was directed, and to a
lesser degree to the United States and Hawaii, where a little more than a third
of the remaining emigrants ended up.[142] Although incomplete, these records
substantiate general observations made concerning the destination of Azorean
emigrants as early as the 1880s.

The stream of emigration from the three most eastern islands of São Miguel, Santa Maria and Terceira,
has through accidental circumstances generally

[142] Graves, "Immigrants in Agriculture," P. 42.

proceeded steadily to Brazil, whereas that from the westernmost islands of Faial, San Jorge and Flores is directed mainly to the United States, whilst Madeira, singularly enough, contributes a by no means insignificant quota to the Sandwich Islands....[143]

Emigration records, at best, give only a general indication of the scale of the migration that took place at the end of the 19th and beginning of the 20th century. They are even worse when used to determine precise points of origin. Even the decennial censuses of the United States, which are the most accurate source of information on the number of foreign born Portuguese residing in this country, at least through 1960, provide little useful information on whether the Portuguese immigrant came from the Azores or the mainland. In the earlier censuses, 1870-1900, a separate category for the Atlantic Islands included part of the Azoreans, depending upon whether the census enumerator listed that as a separate category or, more typically, included Azoreans under Portugal. In more recent years, 1930 for example, the Azores were listed as a separate category; again though, the majority of Azoreans were usually grouped under the category of Portugal and rightfully so.

One estimate of the origin of Portuguese emigrants bound for the United States in the years 1892-1912, based on Portuguese records, concluded that 63 percent were from the Azores Islands, 26 percent from mainland Portugal, and about 11 percent from the Madeira Islands.[144] Most studies that can be related to the Portuguese within the United States, have estimated that Azoreans constitute somewhere between two-thirds and three-fourths of all Portuguese in this country. The remainder are primarily from the mainland and, to a much lesser degree, from the Madeira Islands. Within the United States, there are also significant regional differences. The most recent study of Portuguese in California concluded that they are "almost exclusively of Azorean descent. Most Portuguese Californians are, in fact, from but five of the nine islands of the Azores — Pico, Faial, Flores, San Jorge and Terceira".[145] The Portuguese immigrants to Hawaii were primarily from the Madeira Islands and the island of São Miguel in the Azores. In the continental United States, emigrants from São Miguel

---

[143] Walker, *The Azores or Western Islands,* Pp. 107-108.

[144] Graves, "Immigrants in Agriculture," P. 89.

[145] *Ibid,* P. 158.

remained almost exclusively on the east coast, particularly in Massachusetts, Rhode Island, and Connecticut, as did those from mainland Portugal and the Madeira Islands.

The best information available on the total number of Portuguese immigrants admitted to this country is the data collected by the United States Bureau of Immigration. Prior to 1870, many of the Azoreans who arrived, primarily as crewmen on whaling vessels and as deserters to the gold fields in California, were not enumerated, but after that date the reliability improves greatly. After 1870, the bulk of the Portuguese immigrants relied on the more traditional modes of transportation: packet ships,[146] cargo and passenger ships between Europe and the east coast and finally, steamships operating directly between the Azores and New England for the exclusive purpose of transporting immigrants. The advertisements of these steamship companies promised fast, reliable service between the Azores and the United States. In 1911 the steamship *Venezia,* for example, was advertised as the only one providing monthly service directly between the city of Angra, on the island of Terceira, and the United States. In addition to good accommodations and guaranteed treatment, the company promised the best voyage of the time and only five and one-half days to reach the United States. The same advertisement also offered to provide rail transportation on the most rapid line from the east coast to California. Such arrangements were a far cry from the earlier period when men spent two or three years working their way to the United States on a whaling ship. The prospects of a relatively fast, pleasant trip to join family members already in America encouraged many who were inclined to emigrate but were reluctant to travel.

After 1870, the pace of Portuguese immigration to the United States quickened steadily until 1900 and then was followed by almost twenty years of rapid escalation (*See,* Table 5). Sixty-two percent of all Portuguese immigrants who came to the United States between 1820 and 1930 arrived in the twenty years between 1900 and 1920. As one immigrant commented about coming to the United States in 1903,

> It was easy to get into this country in those early days. America was a free port. To get in, all you needed was a little money in your pocket, so that the

---

[146] Morrison, *The Maritime History of Massachusetts,* pp. 231-232. "A packetline meant two or more vessels whose owners advertised sailing to designated ports, on schedules as regular as wind and weather permitted; and which depended for their profit on freight and passengers furnished by the public rather than goods shipped on the owner's account".

TABLE 5

PORTUGUESE IMMIGRATION TO THE UNITED STATES
1820-1930

Decade	Aggregate	Percent of Total
1820-1830	180	0.1
1831-1840	829	0.3
1841-1850	550	0.2
1851-1860	1,055	0.4
1861-1870	2,658	1.1
1871-1880	14,082	5.6
1881-1890	16,978	6.7
1891-1900	27,508	10.9
1901-1910	69,149	27.3
1911-1920	89,732	35.5
1921-1930	29,994	11.9
TOTAL	252,715	100.0

Source: *Immigration and Naturalization Service, 1976 Annual Report.*
Table 13, pp. 86-88. Washington, D.C.

authorities could be sure that you wouldn't be des-
titute and on relief right away.[147]

In the absence of any restrictive legislation, the total number of immigrants
undoubtedly would have continued to increase during the 1920s. A growing
nativist movement developed in the United States in the 1880s, fueled by
labor unrest in the industrial centers and a growing concern that America
was becoming overcrowded and changing too rapidly. "The beginning of
significant southern and eastern European immigration, and the onset of
economic depression in 1893, made the danger seem more acute".[148] Many

[147] Oliver, *Never Backward,* P. 13.

[148] Taylor, *The Distant Magnet,* P. 243.

perceived these new immigrants as "inferior, peculiarly unfitted to contribute to American society"[149] and, in fact, as a threat to their vision of the traditional American society. Agitation to curtail, or at least restrict, this tide of "undesirable" immigrants increased and finally was rewarded by the establishment of a literacy requirement for all immigrants in 1917. By overwhelming majorities the Congress decided to set immigrants over sixteen a short passage to read in a language of their choice.[150] Illiteracy thereby became the first means of substantially reducing the flow of immigration.

The literacy requirement was exceptionally onerous for the Portuguese immigrants who came from a rural, nonindustrial, agrarian society which offered little, if any, incentive for its members to acquire even a rudimentary education. The rate of illiteracy among Portuguese immigrants over 14, who entered the United States between 1899 and 1917, ranged from a high in 1907 of 76.5 percent to a low in 1915 of 54.2 percent. For the nineteen-year period, illiteracy averaged 63.3 percent.[151] The impact of the new legislation was immediate and severe. In 1916, 12,208 Portuguese immigrants were admitted to the United States; by 1918 the number of immigrants had declined to 2,319 and the following year only 1,574 were allowed in.[152]

Like immigrants the world over, the Portuguese coming to this country were primarily men and women in the prime of their lives. Seventy-three percent of the immigrants arriving between 1899 and 1917 were in the 14-44 age group, twenty percent were under fourteen, while those forty-five and older accounted for only seven percent.[153] The Portuguese who came to America were not fleeing from religious or political oppression; they were seeking an opportunity to improve themselves economically and were willing and capable of working hard to achieve that aim. Letters from friends and relatives living in America vividly described the opportunities awaiting the individual willing to work; those letters together with the stories spun by returned emigrants may have been exaggerated at times but they spurred the flow of new immigrants. It became "almost a habit, in the Azores, to emigrate to the United States."[154]

[149] *Ibid.*

[150] *Ibid.*, P. 247.

[151] Taft, *Two Portuguese Communities in New England,* P. 116.

[152] *Ibid.*, P. 101.

[153] *Ibid.*

[154] *Ibid.*, P. 95.

In the early stages of the Portuguese migration to the United States, prior to 1870, the immigrants were predominantly male. This was, in large part, a reflection of their unusual method of arriving in this country — mainly as sailors on whaling vessels. By 1900, when the flow of immigrants had increased markedly and the mode of transportation was more traditional, Azorean women were also coming to the United States in substantial numbers. Between 1900 and 1919, the ratio of male to female emigrants was approximately three to two.[155] There were no restrictions on women leaving their homeland; they were not subject to conscription and therefore not required to post a bond or resort to clandestine departures. The demand for female labor to work in the cotton mills of Fall River, New Bedford and Providence made it relatively easy for them to find employment and, by 1900, there was a sufficiently large Portuguese population in those cities to ensure that finding a relative or acquaintance to stay with was not a substantial problem. Some women came to the United States to marry their future husband who sent for them, while others came to join family members who had emigrated earlier. Once here, women were much less likely to return to their native islands than were men. For every woman who left the United States to return home between 1908 and 1919 three men also departed.[156]

The rapid rise in the number of Portuguese immigrants arriving after 1900 was accompanied by a steady increase in emigrants leaving the United States to return home. It was common practice for young men who had immigrated to America to work until they could save enough money to return to the Azores and take a wife. Many returned immediately with their new bride; others remained in the islands hoping to use their accumulated capital to become successful farmers or merchants. Some were successful; others watched their money dwindling away and reluctantly decided to return to the United States — only this time accompanied by a wife and children. Still others returned to marry a wife only to find that she refused to leave her family and were themselves forced to remain in the islands. Such was the case with one man who left the islands in his youth as a crewman on a whaler and ended up working in the Central Valley of California for eighteen years. Finally able to realize his dream of returning to his homeland to marry and raise a family, he found that the land of his youth had changed. Unable to persuade his wife to leave the islands, he spent the remainder of his life there. His children, however, followed their father's

[155] *Ibid.,* P. 102.

[156] *Ibid.,* P. 101.

earlier example and immigrated to California.[157] There were also those who returned to the Azores with the intention of staying and found that they could no longer adjust to the slow pace of village life and soon departed again.[158] Their counterparts found life in the United States lacking in many of the traditional values which they had acquired as Azoreans and soon decided that they preferred the lifestyle of their homeland to that of America. They returned at the first opportunity. In the twelve years between 1908 and 1919, no less than 20,751 Portuguese migrated from the United States.[159] Emigration fluctuated with conditions in the United States, and ranged from a low of 816 in 1909 to a high of 3,525 in 1919. Of those emigrating from the United States between 1909 and 1919, 68.9 percent had been in this country five years or less, 24.9 percent between five and ten years, 4.1 percent from ten to fifteen and only 2.1 percent of those leaving had lived here for more than fifteen years.[160]

Undoubtedly the war which was raging in Europe had some influence on the decline in immigration, although it did not appear to noticeably affect emigration during this time. The war did, however, fuel the nativist movement at home which was demanding still more restrictive immigration legislation. In 1921, the Three Percent Law was enacted; it established a quota on the number of immigrants admitted from a particular country at three percent of the residents from that country living in the United States in 1910. The Portuguese annual quota, based on that formula, was substantially reduced to 2,520.[161] The Three Percent Law was followed by more restrictive legislation in 1924; the end result of the new legislation was

> to cut the total immigration, to ensure that European immigration did not much exceed that from the Americas, and to impose drastic cuts in the movement from southern and eastern Europe.[162]

America was no longer the "free port" for immigrants the world over.

---

[157] An interview with Alexandrinha Alves in Patterson, California on November 25, 1878. Her father lived in the United States 18 years before he returned to the Azores and married her mother.

[158] Henriques, *A Trip to the Azores or Western Islands,* P. 104.

[159] Taft, *Two Portuguese Communities in New England,* P. 101.

[160] *Ibid.,* P. 117.

[161] *Ibid.,* P. 102.

[162] Taylor, *The Distant Magnet,* P. 255.

Chapter V

Ethnic Survival: The Maintenance of Cultural Values

Azoreans, like all other people, were a product of their physical and cultural environments, and when they migrated to America their cultural heritage accompanied them like so many pieces of baggage. Given the nature of their interrelatedness and social interaction in their homeland, it was neither unexpected nor unusual that those ties, which constituted their social networks, would direct a chain migration of new immigrants to locations inhabited by fellow Portuguese. It would have been unusual if that had not occurred. Portuguese settlement patterns in America were a direct outgrowth of the triad of family, community, and church that totally dominated and intertwined Azorean life and, at the same time, these settlement patterns encouraged the retention of traditional cultural practices among the immigrants. Foremost among the factors that contributed to the retention of Portuguese cultural identity was their pattern of settlement in this country.

As an ethnic group, the Portuguese were never significant, in terms of absolute numbers, in the total population of the nation, but in certain areas on the east and west coast of the United States they were quite important regionally, and in fact were the dominant ethnic group in a number of communities. The concentration of Portuguese immigrants and their offspring in a relatively small number of locations facilitated the continued utilization of their native language, provided a pool of suitable marriage partners for young adults, and enabled their community to ignore the developing social services in this country and continue, in times of need, their own tradition of self-help. During the first stage of migration, when a Portuguese family was beset by illness, an accident or death, it was common to take up a collection in the community to help those in need. Meager though such donations were, they generally sufficed to bury the dead and provide temporary assistance to the living. A number of fraternal and mutual aid societies gradually evolved out of these early efforts to help one another; one of the earliest was the *Associacāo Portuguesa Protectora e Beneficente,* (Portuguese Protective and Benevolent Society) which was formed in San Francisco on July 6, 1868. Its primary function was "to protect the living and bury the dead."[163] In addition to the mutual aid funds, which went to the widow and children of the deceased, these early fraternal societies dignified the burial of the immigrant, usually with a simple ceremony at the cemetery, and rendered aid and sympathy to the bereaved.[164] Branches of the Portuguese Protective and Benevolent Society soon appeared in other communities in the bay area; Hayward, for example, formed a branch in March, 1870, while San Leandro's appeared in July of the same year.[165]

Initially, most of these fraternal and mutual aid societies, like the *Uniāo Portuguese do Estado da California* (Portuguese Union of the State of California) or U.P.E.C. as it was commonly known after its founding in San Leandro in 1880, would assess their surviving members $1.00 each, upon notification of the death of a member; the size of the paying membership determined the amount that went to the deceased's family. The variation in benefits and the cumbersome nature of the collection process resulted in efforts to standardize both costs and benefits, and the societies were gradually transformed into a system of regular insurance coverage. By 1892 members of the U.P.E.C., for example, were paying regular monthly dues which insured that, when they died, their beneficiary would receive a set amount of money.[166] The benefits of belonging to such an organization were readily apparent to all and membership in the various societies flourished. Local branches of the fraternal organizations appeared in Portuguese communities on both coasts of the United States and by 1918, the U.P.E.C., which was just one of several Portuguese fraternal societies in California, had 12,491 paying members.[167]

[163] August Mark Vaz, *The Portuguese in California* (Oakland, 1965), P. 82.

[164] *Ibid.,* P. 80.

[165] Halley, *The Centennial Year Book of Alameda County, California,* P.292.

[166] Vaz, *The Portuguese in California,* P. 91.

[167] Cardozo, *The Portuguese in America 1590 BC-1974,* P. 34.

Membership in the early fraternal societies was exclusively for males, but in 1898 the *Sociedade Portuguesa Rainha Santa Isabel* (Portuguese Society of Queen Saint Isabel) was founded. The S.P.R.S.I., as it was obviously referred to, was formed as a ladies' society to serve as a focal point for cultural and charitable activities among the Portuguese; it also provided a standard insurance benefit for its members. The number of chapters increased rapidly and the S.P.R.S.I. became the most prestigious Portuguese women's organization in the United States. As late as 1974 it still had 13,500 members.[168]

While the mutual aid benefits provided financial assistance to the survivors of deceased members, the fraternal aspects of the societies were enjoyed by the living. As the organizations became more formalized, local chapters held regular monthly business meetings; the meetings were complete with the election and installation of local officers and the selection of delegates to attend the annual regional and statewide meetings. These local meetings, which were conducted in Portuguese, were as much social as business affairs, and were instrumental in maintaining interaction within the Portuguese community. The annual meetings, which were filled with pomp and ceremony designed to instill a sense of pride in being Portuguese, were occasions for the immigrant population to reaffirm ties with friends and relatives living in other communities and for their children to associate with other young Portuguese people. While the meetings and social activities of the fraternal societies were instrumental in reinforcing the cultural values of the community and retaining the use of the Portuguese language outside of the home, they also performed another important function.

> It was the various societies, with their rituals and social activities which often added color and ceremony to break the monotonous pattern of daily life and enriched the social life of the individual and the family.[169]

Color and enrichments were noticeably absent from the lives of most immigrants in the United States in the early 1900s. The difficult times which the Manuel A. family of California experienced in the 1920s and 1930s were shared by their urban counterparts working in the

[168] *Ibid.,* Pp. 46-47.

[169] Vaz, *The Portuguese in California,* P. 80.

mills and sweat shops of New England. If anything, conditions were even
worse for the city dwellers who were completely dependent upon earning an
income to provide for their family. Rural inhabitants could at least grow part
of their own food supply when jobs were scarce, and urban jobs in New
England mill towns became noticeably scarce after the mid-1920s. The
increasing unionization of the textile industry in New England, together with
the growing obsolescence of much of the original mill equipment, made that
industry particularly susceptible to competition from modern textile mills
that were locating in the South to take advantage of low-cost, non-union
labor. As the economic realities of the industry became more apparent, some
mill owners accepted what they saw as the inevitability of the situation,
closed their New England plants and joined the move to the South in search
of cheap labor. Others tried to forestall the impending crisis by cutting wages
in their existing plants; the workers, caught in the middle of a situation which
they neither created nor understood, reacted by striking. In the textile mills
of New Bedford, for example—and they were by no means atypical—
management announced a ten percent wage cut in 1928 and the mill
workers reacted by going out on strike. The strike lasted six months, the
longest and most severe strike in the city's history, and only succeeded in
aggravating a deteriorating situation.[170]

Already reeling under the intense competition from
the South, the depression of the 1930s dealt the textile industry of New
England the final blow. New Bedford lost two-thirds of its cotton textile mills
during the depression and became "a typical example of a depressed
one-industry city."[171] The number of wage earners employed in cotton
textiles in New Bedford between 1927 and 1938, decreased by 21,280.[172]
Hampered by their lack of education and delayed acquisition of English as a
second language, "fully ninety-one percent of their workers (Portuguese)
were found in the semi-skilled and unskilled occupations"[173] which bore the
brunt of the layoffs and job terminations that swept the New England textile
industries during the thirties. Ill-prepared to compete on the open job
market, the Portuguese suffered from high rates of unemployment; half of the
Portuguese working population of New Bedford, for example, were left

[170] Wolfbein, *The Decline of a Cotton Textile City*, P. 11.

[171] *Ibid.*, P. 12.

[172] *Ibid.*, P. 125.

[173] *Ibid.*, P. 44.

without jobs during the thirties.[174] As a study by the International Labor
Office reported in 1937, New Bedford was not alone.

> The movement of cotton manufacturing to the South
> has created in New England (in such cities as New
> Bedford, Fall River and Lowell, and especially in the
> smaller towns) a serious problem of more or less
> permanently "stranded population"...[175]

Portuguese workers were particularly conspicuous in
that "stranded population" and were hard hit by their economic misfortune.
At the same time that the textile industry was responding to cheaper labor
cost in the South by relocating to that region, the garment industry of New
York City was trying to escape their increasing labor costs. Historically
dependent upon low-cost, unskilled, immigrant labor, the garment industry
was affected by the decline in new immigrants after 1924 and viewed their
rising labor costs with apprehension. New York City's importance as the
fashion center of the United States dictated that the garment industry, while
not tied exclusively to the city, remain in relatively close proximity. Lower
production costs in New Jersey and Connecticut and the increasing pool of
unemployed workers in southern Massachusetts stimulated a substantial
migration of the garment industry from New York City to those areas after
the late 1920s. In New Bedford, the clothing industry was the third-ranking
employer in terms of toal number of employees, by 1938.[176]

During this period many Portuguese immigrants,
who had previously worked in the textile mills, sought employment in the
garment industry. Unskilled and uneducated, they were ideal candidates for
the low-paying job of mass producing clothing. Even so, the new industry
was not able to substantially reduce unemployment among Portuguese
workers in Fall River and New Bedford and "many of them moved to
Newark, New Jersey, and other cities in search of jobs".[177] The early stages of
the migration from Massachusetts to Connecticut and New Jersey were
already apparent in the Census of 1930 (*See* Table 5). These early migrants,
like their predecessors who first came to America, established themselves in

[174] *Ibid.*

[175] *Ibid.,* Pp. 28-29.

[176] *Ibid.,* Pp. 115-116.

[177] Pap, *Portuguese American Speech,* P. 14.

urban occupations and provided a destination and assistance to subsequent waves of migration during the thirties.

The economic malaise which settled on the New England textile centers in the 1920s slowed the occupational progress of its newest immigrant groups to a standstill; this was particularly true for the Portuguese in places like Fall River and New Bedford where that progress has remained stalled to the present.[178] In addition to making it difficult to maintain family and community stability, the loss of jobs and continued unemployment had a negative impact upon traditional Portuguese cultural values among some members of the community who came to associate "being Portuguese" with being unemployable or somehow inferior to being American. The move to disassociate themselves, at least from the more visible signs of their cultural heritage, such as speaking Portuguese, became more commonplace. As one researcher commented in 1949:

> Many Portuguese immigrants and their children have leaned toward discarding the Portuguese language, only in order to conceal their background as a means means of overcoming social prejudices, but also in order to fulfill what they consider a patriotic duty.[179]

The immigrant's life was a radical departure from the traditional lifestyle of the Azores; invariably, everything seemed to be done differently in America and immigrants had little choice but to adapt. In the process of changing and making innumerable adjustments to life in this new world, many traditional practices were quietly abandoned by the wayside. In the midst of all the turmoil and uncertainty, however, the Church stood constant and unchanging and provided a welcome sense of security. A shared faith in the Roman Catholic Church was the most basic component of the Portuguese cultural heritage and the one most resistant to change. Immigrants and their children might give up their native language, anglicize their family name, and divorce themselves of everything that identified them as Portuguese, but they rarely gave up their religion. For the vast majority, it was a religion based on simple faith; uneducated, they were not versed in the doctrine of the church but rather in the ritual. From the peasant perspective, it was not necessary to understand the tenets of the church as long as one had faith and followed the religious dictates of the priest. Bordering on mysti-

---

[178] Silva, "The Position of 'New' Immigrants in the Fall River Textile Industry," Pp. 231-232.

[179] Pap, *Portuguese American Speech,* P. 25.

cism, their religion combined an inordinate faith in the power of saints with a strict devotion to the ritual and ceremony of the mass.

Millions of other immigrants were also adherents of the Catholic faith, particularly those from southern Europe, and the Church was already well established in America when most of the Portuguese arrived. Regional variations exist in all institutions, even in those religious institutions professing the same basic doctrines, and the Portuguese preferred their churches in America to be similar, both in ritual and appearance, to the ones they left behind in the Azores. A Portuguese priest was first sent to New Bedford in 1867 to care for the religious needs of the Portuguese immigrants concentrated there[180] and when sizeable Portuguese communities became established in other cities, such as Fall River, Providence, and San Leandro, they continued the practice of seeking priests who were familiar with their cultural heritage and could speak their native language. Although the total number of Portuguese speaking priests was never very large, the concentrated settlement patterns of Portuguese immigrants made it possible for a limited number of priests to maintain contact with a substantial body of immigrants. Outlying communities that were unable to have a permanent Portuguese priest of their own had, to be satisfied with a visiting Portuguese priest, who came from the nearby cities, to say the mass for the local *festa* and for other special occasions.

In addition to a preference for Portuguese speaking priests, many of the Catholic Churches built in Portuguese communities were modeled after churches in their homeland. While the architecture often brought back memories of the old village churches, the interior always contained the familiar symbols, particularly the images of the saints, so associated with their religion in the Azores. When all else failed, the Church remained the one continuous link with the past and "strove to remind the immigrant of his faith and struggled to keep the faith alive in the face of countless obstacles".[181]

Closely related to the Church, is the system of godparentage which is itself a fundamental institution in the Portuguese community. At the time of baptism every infant needs a godmother and a godfather to serve as sponsor; traditionally parents invited a brother, sister

---

[180] Taft, *Two Portuguese Communities in New England*, P. 97.

[181] Vaz, *The Portuguese in California*, P. 19.

or a very close friend to be godparents to their children. While the primary
function was to ensure the religious training of the child, becoming a godparent
also established a special relationship, not just between the godparents and
the child, but with the child's natural parents as well. In the traditional
Portuguese society, an intricate system of community ties and relationships,
only marginally related to the church, evolved from the religious need for
godparents. These relationships were based on mutual obligations, re-
sponsibilties and rights and further strengthened and expanded the normal
family bonds. In times of crisis an individual's *compadres,* the godparents of
his children and the parents of his godchildren,could always be relied upon
for comfort and assistance; they also joined in and helped celebrate the more
memorable occasions that occur in every family.

It was not uncommon for immigrants to have to
borrow money to pay their passage to America and they frequently turned to
parents, siblings and compadres for such assistance. After securing a job and
a place to live, they saved their money, repaid the loan, and encouraged
others to join them. Well aware of the meager existence that was the fate of
most people in the Azores, they felt a strong sense of obligation to help those
closest to them — brothers, sisters, parents and compadres. After a second
member of the family immigrated and found work, they customarily pooled
their resources to help those left behind come to the United States. In this
way, entire extended families took part in chain migrations from their
homeland to a particular community in this country. The ties that helped
maintain traditional Azorean society, family, church, and community, were
reinforced and transported with them, but the role of the godparent, which
combines both religious and family ties, suffered in the subsquent assimilation
process. Although the special relationship between compadres and between
godparents and godchildren remained intact for the immigrants and their
children, its significance began to decline with the third generation and by
the fourth generation being a godparent was little more than a religious
ceremony.

All Portuguese immigrants brought their cultural
heritage with them to America, but the Portuguese in California were the
most successful in retaining that heritage and passing it on to subsequent
generations. Where the new immigrants settled and what occupations they
ended up in, which was largely determined by the social connections between
prospective immigrants and those already in America, were the key factors
that influenced the length of time that cultural traits were retained. For
reasons already noted, most of the Portuguese immigrants who settled on the

east coast ended up working as semi-skilled or unskilled factory laborers in cities like Fall River and New Bedford, Massachusetts, and Providence, Rhode Island. In 1960, eighty-seven percent of the Portuguese in southeastern New England were city residents and only one percent were working as agriculturalists of any type.[182] It was only in California that a large number of Portuguese settled and remained on farms. Eighty-seven percent of all the Portuguese farm residents in the United States in 1960 were living in California where the Portuguese have remained the most rural ethnic group in the state since the close of immigration in the early 1920s.[183] The predominantly rural nature of Portuguese settlement in California isolated the immigrants culturally as well as spatially and, as a consequence, minimized the contact between Portuguese immigrants and the non-Portuguese members of the host society. Almost the exact opposite occurred in the industrial centers in New England, where Portuguese immigrants,

> were forced to go outside their group and domestic circle, to work in the factories in subordinate positions, thus having to learn some English or remain in low manual jobs where little or no communication was needed.[184]

This is not to say that the Portuguese immigrants in New England abandoned their cultural heritage when they stepped off the boat from the Azores. Nothing could be farther from the truth. What it does indicate, however, is that the cultural conflict, which inevitably results when members of different groups are forced into close juxtaposition, occurred on the east coast long before it began to be obvious among second and third generation Portuguese in California. In Hawaii, the de-emphasis of the Portuguese cultural heritage was an almost immediate reaction among the immigrants themselves when they perceived that the visible signs of that heritage, *i.e.,* language, occupation and social practices, made them targets for discrimination. As early as 1941, it was noted that,

> there is a wide cultural differentiation between the Portuguese in the Island setting and those in California today. Although there have been changes in cultural patterns of the Portuguese in California, it is

[182] Graves, "Immigrants in Agriculture," Pp. 10-11.

[183] *Ibid.,* Pp. 11-12.

[184] Pap, *Portuguese American Speech,* P. 13.

in Hawaii, where the Portuguese people have gone through the process of competition, conflict, accommodation, and assimilation and have broken down social distance, that the distinction from the old world pattern is most evident.[185]

The economic rewards associated with agriculture in California were a marked contrast to the situation in Hawaii; immigrants were drawn to the rural areas in the former and fled from them in the latter. The lack of day-to-day contact with people, other than one's own family, the need to be self-sufficient, the general unavailability of many amenities common in urban areas, and the general sense of isolation that are commonly associated with rural life in the first half of the 20th century were conditions conducive to the continuation of old world traditions among Portuguese immigrants in California.

Summer was a great time to be Portuguese in California. A festa, or celebration, was held almost every weekend in some community in the Central Valley or along the coast and everyone looked forward to the occasion; it was a time for dancing, eating and socializing. Traditionally, every Portuguese community of any size would hold an annual celebration. Most of these were two-day affairs which began with a candlelight procession on Saturday night. The procession transported the queen's crown from the house of the sponsoring family to a chapel in or near the church; afterwards a dance was held in the local Portuguese Hall where the chamarita, a traditional folk dance, shared the floor with less traditional dances. The following day a parade, complete with suitably gowned outgoing and incoming queens, participants from fraternal organizations in all nearby towns, and statues of saints from the church, would transport the queen's crown from the chapel, through town, and end up at the church where the participants attended mass. At the conclusion of mass, the crown would be blessed, the new queen crowned and the procession would march back to the chapel. Afterwards a traditional meal of meat and bread was served free to the public.[186]

The local Portuguese celebration remained visible in California long after it ceased to exist in most New England and Hawaiian

[185] Estep, "Portuguese Assimilation in Hawaii and California," P. 64.

[186] Diane Amaral Lane, "Portuguese Religious Festivals" (Unpublished M.A. Thesis, California State University, Chico, 1978), Pp. 22-23.

communities. It contributed to the maintenance of strong ties among the Portuguese population by facilitating the exchange of news and information among the members of a rural population and transmitting the cultural traditions of the immigrants to their children. The children were just as much a part of the festivities as adults; they learned to dance the chamarita, marched in the procession, and enjoyed the afternoon meal as much as their parents. In the process, they grew up accustomed to hearing Portuguese used as the common language not only at home but at the social functions they attended. They also had ample opportunities to become acquainted with boys and girls who shared their cultural heritage. As one writer noted in 1941,

> proud of their old-world background, their language, and their institutions, the Portuguese in California have sought to pass these things on to their children.[187]

In 1932 a group of Portuguese from Gustine, a small San Joaquin Valley town on the west side of Stanislaus County, decided to start a special celebration to attract Portuguese from all over California. They modeled their celebration on one which is held in the Azores, on the island of Terceira, and called it *Nossa Senhora dos Milagres* (Our Lady of Miracles). In contrast to the traditional two-day festa, the Gustine celebration quickly evolved into a full week of activities including: candlelight processions, nightly prayers at the Catholic church, the blessing of cows and distribution of milk and Portuguese sweet bread, music and songs performed by Portuguese musicians, a Saturday night dance, an elaborate version of the traditional Sunday procession to and from the church, mass said by a visiting priest brought over from the Azores, an auction to raise money to help support the celebration, a carnival for children, a Sunday night dance, and, finally, on Monday, a bloodless bullfight copied after those held on the island of Terceira.[188]

While many of the local festas have atrophied and gradually disappeared, leaving behind only a somewhat dilapidated Portuguese Hall vaguely to remind third and fourth generation Portuguese-Americans of their cultural heritage, the festas in the larger Portuguese communities in California are still commonplace. None, however, can compare to the Our Lady of Miracles celebration at Gustine; it has become a

---

[187]   Estep, "Portuguese Assimilation in Hawaii and California," P. 68.

[188]   Lane, "Portuguese Religious Festivals," Pp. 65-77.

social event without par for the Portuguese population of California. In 1977, an estimated twenty-eight thousand people crowded into the small town of Gustine to help celebrate the annual Our Lady of Miracles festival. Forty-six Portuguese communities, some over 150 miles away, sent representatives, in the form of the queen of their celebration or members of their sponsoring fraternal organizations, to march in the parade on Sunday. They were accompanied by twenty decorated statues, the local queen and her attendants, all suitably gowned and robed, and six marching bands. All in all it was a gala event which, though it cost in excess of fifty thousand dollars to stage, generated over one hundred thousand dollars in revenues. The local Catholic Church, the thankful recipient of most of the profits from the festival, is prospering; the community is justifiably proud of its festival; Portuguese statewide look forward to the fall event; and the celebration continues to draw more participants each year.[189]

The east coast counterpart of the Our Lady of Miracles festival is seen in the Blessing of the Fleet in Gloucester and Provincetown, The Feast of the Blessed Sacrament in New Bedford, and the Feast of the Holy Ghost in New Bedford and Fall River, all of which attract large enthusiastic crowds. It is primarily in California, though, where the rural-based Portuguese communities have continued to support their local festas as well as the more elaborate Our Lady of Miracles. The survival of the festa, along with other cultural traditions, has been most tenuous in the Hawaiian Islands. Almost forty years ago it was noted that "Religious and fraternal festivals play a far greater part in the lives of California Portuguese than is the case with their brothers in Hawaii".[190] Their decline in Hawaii has become even more accentuated in the ensuing forty years.

One of the earliest casualties of the acculturation process was the Portuguese language. It persisted the longest in large, urban Portuguese communities where many immigrants, particularly women not employed outside the home, were able to get by without learning English, and in the rural communities where there was little social or economic interaction with the English speaking population. In the rural areas of California, for example, immigrants could get along quite well without learning English and, in fact, many of them never learned the language. At work and in the home Portuguese was always spoken; on Sundays, the

[189] *Ibid.,* Pp. 74-77.

[190] Estep, "Portuguese Assimilation in Hawaii and California," P. 65.

liturgy of the mass at the local Catholic Church was performed in Latin — as it had been in their homeland, and in some communities the sermon was delivered in Portuguese. The major social events, the summer festas in nearby town or the meetings of the fraternal organizations were also occasions to converse in Portuguese. Although the children learned English in school, they were frequently informed that speaking English stopped at the outside door to the house.

The acculturation process weighed most heavily upon children of immigrant parents — the second generation. Forced, by law, to attend school where their lessons and social interactions with non-Portuguese children were carried on in English, they learned to speak that language away from home while they continued to communicate with their parents in Portuguese. While many immigrants never learned English, their children became bilingual, at least to the degree of being able to function in either language. It was these children of immigrants, born in the United States and seldom formally taught Portuguese, "who were mainly responsible for the origin, use and propagation of anglicisms and for the deterioration of Portuguese in general".[191]

The bastardization of the Portuguese language in California took many forms, but it primarily consisted of using an English word, with Portuguese pronunciation, to express a concept or object totally new to the immigrant; using an English word that sounded similar to a well known Portuguese word, although with an entirely different meaning; and, translating English into Portuguese literally on a word-for-word basis. Each of these frequently results in a spoken language which at best confuses the Portuguese speaking newcomer and frequently either amuses or embarrasses that individual because the meaning in contemporary Portuguese is something quite different from that expressed in California Portuguese.[192] In spite of their linguistic deficiencies, second generation Portuguese were quite capable of making themselves understood in either English or Portuguese and they continued the practice of speaking Portuguese whenever they were with other members of their own generation. They spoke it less frequently with their own children, however, who were rapidly being acculturated into the larger society.

[191] Francisco Cota Fagundes, "O Falar Luso-Americano: Un Indice de Acculturacao," *First Symposium on Portuguese Presence in California* (San Franciso, 1974) p. 17. My translation of the quote.

[192] *Ibid.,* Pp. 8-17.

The third generation became, for all practical pur-
poses, unilingual, English speaking Portuguese Americans. Although they
frequently understood some Portuguese, from hearing their parents and
grandparents converse and from attending Portuguese celebrations, most
were not able to communicate effectively in their grandparents' language.[193]
On the east coast of the United States, where urban living brought the
immigrants and their children into daily contact with the English speaking
community, the process of learning English was frequently much more rapid.
In the Hawaiian Islands acculturation was even more accelerated than it
was on the east coast as the Portuguese hurried to disband as a nationality
group.

A more subtle way in which the passing years have
eroded the Portuguese cultural traditions has been through the increasing
incidence of out-marriage, particularly among third and fourth generation
Portuguese Americans. The habit of seeking marriage partners from their
homeland, and frequently from their own village, as reported earlier in the
discussion of Rhode Island, was common practice among Portuguese
immigrants throughout the United States. The social interactions of the
immigrants through their churches, fraternal organizations and celebrations
ensured that most of the second generation found marriage partners within
the Portuguese community. Again, the Hawaiian Islands were the main
exception. In the late 1930s, 36.2 percent of the Portuguese males and 51.4
percent of the females were reported marrying outside their own ethnic
group; in contrast, ten percent were estimated to be marrying outside their
group in California at that time.[194]

It is among the third generation, and those that
followed, that marrying non-Portuguese Americans has, understandably,
become rather common. The third generation, typically, can neither speak
nor understand Portuguese sufficiently well to be at ease in a Portuguese
speaking situation and are less likely to be actively involved in fraternal
organizations, celebrations, and other social activities as their parents were
as young adults. As a consequence, they are unlikely to interact socially with
many suitable marriage partners who share their cultural heritage. Instead,
most of their social activities, from the time they first enter the public school

---

[193] Geoffrey L. Gomes, "Bilingualism Among Second and Third Generation Portuguese-
Americans in California," *First Symposium on Portuguese Presence in California* (San Francisco, 1974), P. 45.

[194] Estep, "Portuguese Assimilation in Hawaii and California," P. 63.

system, tend to be predominantly with English speaking non-Portuguese young people. By the time they are old enough to start considering marriage, sharing a cultural heritage is not necessarily a high priority in choosing a partner. Those who marry outside the group were seldom active in the social activities of the Portuguese community before they wed and are less likely to be actively involved afterwards. The use of Portuguese at these activities, frequently not well understood by the Portuguese American member and completely foreign to the non-Portuguese partner, makes it difficult for them to socialize. The offspring of such marriages generally do not learn much of their Portuguese heritage; they do not learn the language; and they are not active participants in the social activities of the group. In short, an almost complete breakdown occurs in the transmission of the traditional Portuguese culture to future generations.

Cultural values are not like an old pair of shoes that can be casually replaced when they are no longer in fashion. The cultural heritage which accompanied the Portuguese immigrants to America had provided the rationale for their very existence in the Azores and, as such, was not easily laid aside for the, as yet, untried traditions in this country. Those same traditions, which were so important to the immigrant, had less meaning, however, for each succeeding generation as they became more assimilated into the host society. While many of the more overt traditions, *i.e.,* speaking Portuguese, active membership in fraternal societies, and particpation in traditional celebrations, are not so common today among Portuguese Americans, many of the basic values of Portuguese society have remained. They still emphasize the importance of the family; the father continues to be the authority figure; and they strive to maintain their ties with the extended family. A study of cultural persistence among a Portuguese community in an urban setting in the early 1960s concluded that

> while the Portuguese American subculture has re-
> mained marginal it has also maintained coherence, in
> contrast not only with most other American subcul-
> tures but also with the general culture of the "receiving
> society".[195]

The Portuguese population of the United States has successfully maintained a strong sense of ethnic identity over an extended

---

[195] Hans Howard Leder, "Cultural Persistence in a Portuguese-American Community" (Unpublished Ph.D Dissertation, Stanford U., 1968), Pp. 88-89.

period of time. The nature of the migration process itself contributed to the maintenance of Portuguese communities and the general feeling of "being Portuguese". Instead of a single mass migration of immigrants who were then widely scattered throughout the country, Portuguese immigrants have continued to come to the same general locations since 1870. The traditional Portuguese cultural values were constantly reinforced by the arrival of new immigrants. In the absence of any new influx of Azorean immigrants, most visible signs of their culture might be expected to disappear gradually. So far, this has not happened because an extended period of non-immigration has yet to occur. The flow of immigrants was severely curtailed as a result of the restrictive legislation of the early 1920s when the Portuguese found, along with immigrants from all over the world, that the portals to America, although not completely closed, were greatly constricted.

A volcanic eruption on the island of Faial in 1957 prompted the first substantial loosening of immigration restrictions for Azoreans. The subsequent Azorean Refugee Acts of 1958 and 1960, which were passed by Congress to make exception for Azoreans suffering from the natural disaster on Faial, was the beginning of the third stage of migration.[196] New immigration legislation enacted in the mid-1960s was much less restrictive and authorized a substantial increase in the number of immigrants permitted to enter the United States from all foreign countries. The impact of the new legislation on Portuguese immigration is reflected in the statistics: in the twenty years prior to 1950 only 10,752 Portuguese migrated to the United States; in the eighteen years between 1961 and 1977 more than 150,000 came to this country — thirty-five percent of the total Portuguese immigration since 1820![197] Traditional Portuguese cultural values, far from being an endangered species, are experiencing a revitalization as a result of the current migration.

[196] Francis M. Rogers, "Americans of Portuguese Descent: A Lesson in Differentiation," *Sage Research Paper in the Social Sciences,* No. 90-013 (Beverly Hills, 1974), P.33.

[197] *Immigration and Naturalization Service, 1976 Annual Report* (Washington, D.C., 1977), Pp. 86-88. Data for 1977 is from correspondence with the Immigration and Naturalization Service in Washington, D.C.

Chapter VI

Too Little for too Many:
The Azorean Dilemma

The second stage of migration, which came to a close between 1920 and 1930, substantially reduced population pressure on the limited resource base of the Azores. The out-migration was not accompanied, however, by any change in the basic social, economic, or political structure of the islands. The overall situation in 1930 was little changed from the mid-1800s: it remained a traditional society interconnected through marriage and god parentage ties; subsistence agriculture still dominated the economy; and, the government in Lisbon continued to treat the islands, politically and economically, as if they were a colony instead of an integral part of the nation. The general economic depression which beset the world during the 1930s virtually ensured that the nature of life in the islands, which had enabled the population to survive difficult times in the past, would remain unchanged. In effect, the "breathing room" which resulted from relieving the population pressure in the islands, was not perceived as an opportunity to bring about needed structural changes, particularly in the economic realm where they were so badly needed, and life continued as usual. Given such conditions, it was inevitable that, in the absence of any significant out-migration, population pressure would begin to increase again and eventually reach crisis proportions; one generation later, in the mid-1950s overpopulation was, once again, the over-riding problem in the Azores.

In 1950 the population of the Azores had climbed to 316,287, an increase of 67,152 individuals in thirty years. A graph depicting the age and sex composition of the population enumerated in the 1950

Census reveals a typical expanding population, with the largest number of people in the younger age groups and each cohort larger than the cohort born before it (*See,* Table 6). In spite of the significant out-migration that took place prior to 1920, the 1950 age-sex pyramid does not have a noticeable gap in any particular cohort of the population, which illustrates both the nature and effectiveness of that earlier migration. Migrations typically are selective, in that they attract primarily the population in the 15-45 age group, and their absence remains visible in an age-sex pyramid until the people in those age groups eventually cease to exist. The absence of any significant gaps in the 1950 age-sex pyramid illustrates again the degree to which the previous migration was a chain migration of interrelated individuals which removed entire, extended families from the Azores — not just young adults.

The still expanding population of the Azores attained an average density of 355 persons per square mile in 1950 and ranged from 570 persons per square mile on São Miguel to 108 on Corvo. Even though it had the largest base population in 1920, São Miguel, through a combination of natural growth and intra-island migration, suffered from a disproportionate share of the new inhabitants; seventy-eight percent (52,422 individuals) of the total population increase in the archipelago was concentrated on São Miguel in 1950 (*See,* Table 7). In a subsistence-agrarian economy, high average population densities are a good indicator of a hand-to-mouth existence and such was certainly the case in the Azores by 1950. In relation to the amount of agricultural land on São Miguel, the actual density of the population exceeded 1,300 per square mile. Limited by the nature of their expanding population, future prospects for the Azoreans appeared rather bleak in 1950. Two unexpected events during the following decade offered a ray of hope in what was becoming a desperate situation: Canada gradually lowered its immigration barriers to selected countries, including Portugal; and a natural disaster, in the form of a volcanic eruption, persuaded the United States to admit Portuguese refugees to this country.

The Portuguese population of Canada was less than 4,000 individuals in 1953 when the Canadian government, in an effort to promote economic development, revised its immigration laws and allowed the first boatload of Portuguese immigrants to enter that country. Most of those early immigrants went to work as agricultural laborers or unskilled construction workers for the railroads. The favorable response, on the part of the Portuguese, to the opportunity to immigrate to Canada, soon prompted

TABLE 6

POPULATION PYRAMID OF THE AZORES—1950

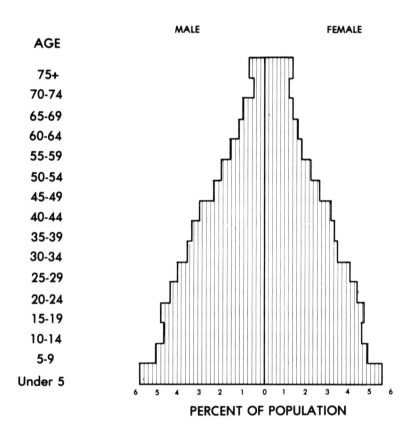

Source: *IX Recenseamento Geral da Populacao No Continente e Ilhas Adjacentes em 15 de Dezembro de 1950, Tomo II, Instituto Nacional de Estatistica, Lisboa, 1952.*

TABLE 7

POPULATION OF THE AZORES 1920-1950

Islands	Pop.[1] 1920	Pop. P/S/M	Pop.[2] 1950	Apparent Change Since 1920	Pop. P/S/M 1950
Santa Maria	6,457	174	11,844	+ 5,387	320
São Miguel	111,745	388	164,167	+52,422	570
Terceira	46,277	302	60,372	+14,092	394
Graciosa	7,477	311	9,517	+ 2,040	396
São Jorge	13,362	145	15,529	+ 2,167	168
Pico	19,927	118	22,557	+ 2,630	134
Faial	18,917	286	23,923	+ 5,006	362
Flores	6,720	122	7,650	+ 930	139
Corvo	661	98	728	+ 67	108
TOTAL	231,543	260	316,287	+67,152	355

Source: [1] *Sumula de Dados Estatistico*, Departamento Regional de Estudios e Planeamento (Acores, 1976), p. 4.

[2] *Populacão dos Acores*, Departamento Regional de Estudios e Planeamento, (Acores, 1975).

the government to increase its original quota of 500 per year.[198] In 1960, there were 22,434 Portuguese immigrants in Canada; ten years later the total reached 84,968.[199] The rush to leave Portugal continued into the 1970s; between 1971 and 1977 another 65,180 Portuguese immigrants arrived in Canada, with 16,333 arriving in 1974 alone.[200] By 1978, Canada was home to some 150,148 Portuguese immigrants — virtually all of whom had arrived since 1953.

Admittedly, the Canadian government's figures are conservative and do not include the illegal Portuguese immigrants living in Canada. A recent study by Grace M. Anderson and David Higgs, *A Future to Inherit: The Portuguese Population of Canada,* estimated the Portuguese population of Canada to be 220,000 in 1976. In particular, the authors took note of the scale of illegal immigration to Canada and the role played by travel agents in both Portugal and Canada in coaching prospective immigrants, for a fee, on how to come to that country on a tourist visa and then remain there illegally.[201] While there may be some question about the actual size of the Portuguese population of Canada, depending on whether one relies on official or unofficial data, it is clearly substantial in number, and recent in origin.

In many ways, the Portuguese immigration to Canada was almost a duplicate of the Portuguese experience in the United States; this was particularly true in such areas as origin, degree of concentration, occupation, and the influence of social ties in determining who would immigrate, where they would end up and what they would do when they got there. Most of the immigrants were from the Azores, about seventy percent and, in contrast to the early arrivals who started out working on farms or for the railroads, the vast majority of them ended up in the city. The city, in this case, was most often Toronto, which by 1978 had a Portuguese community of about 100,000.[202] Second only to Toronto was Montreal with a Portuguese

[198] Caroline B. Brettell, "Ethnicity and Entrepreneurs: Portuguese Immigrants in A Canadian City". In *Ethnic Encounters: Identities and Contexts.* Edited by George L. Hicks and Phillip E. Leis. North Scituate, Mass. 1977. P. 171.

[199] Grace M. Anderson, *Networks of Contact: The Portuguese and Toronto.* Waterloo, Ontario. 1974. P.9.

[200] *Immigration Statistics Canada* (various years 1971-1977). Ottawa, Canada.

[201] Grace M. Anderson and David Higgs, *A Future to Inherit: The Portuguese Communities of Canada.* Toronto. 1976. Pp. 30-32.

[202] Stanley Meisler, "Portuguese in Canada Cling to Old Ways", *Los Angeles Times,* Dec. 5, 1978. P. 20.

community in excess of 20,000.[203] In 1977, ninety-four percent of all the Portuguese immigrants in Canada were concentrated in three provinces: Ontario, with seventy percent; Quebec, sixteen percent; and British Columbia, eight percent.[204] Most of the male immigrants found unskilled jobs as construction workers, custodians in public buildings, or gardeners, while many of the women were employed as domestics or worked in the textile and clothing industries in Toronto.[205] A study of Portuguese immigrants in Toronto found that the decision to go to Toronto was strongly influenced, for the most part, by their contacts with other Portuguese immigrants already living there; most immigrants either found jobs through their contacts in Toronto or relied heavily upon them for information about job opportunities; and, the kinds of jobs that were controlled by an immigrant's network, strongly influenced that immigrant's long-term prospects of achieving job mobility or becoming trapped in a dead-end job.[206] Although Canada has started to tighten its immigration restrictions again, it is still possible for an immigrant to sponsor other family members to Canada. These chain migrations influence what area of Portugal the immigrants come from, keep the flow of immigration coming, and ensure the new immigrants a place to stay and assistance in finding employment.

Culturally, the experience of the Portuguese immigrant in Canada is also similiar to that in the United States. Even though they tend to congregate in cultural enclaves in Toronto and Montreal, most of the immigrants are forced to learn some English on their job and adapt to the Canadian way of doing things. Again, however, it is the children who most quickly learn English and, in spite of the admonitions of their parents, become Canadianized. The dream of migrating to Canada, working for a few years and then returning to the homeland recedes farther into the distance as the children grow up relating less to the old country than to the new one and unwilling to return to a land that becomes more foreign to them with each passing year.[207]

The flow of Portuguese immigrants to the United States never completely ceased after the restrictive legislation of the early

---

[203] Brettell, "Ethnicity and Entrepreneurs". P. 171.

[204] Anderson, *Networks of Contact*. P. 8.

[205] Brettell, "Ethnicity and Entrepreneurs". P. 172.

[206] Anderson, *Networks of Contact*. Pp. xiii-xiv.

[207] Meisler, "Portuguese in Canada Cling to Old Ways".

1920s was enacted, but it came close during the depression years of the 1930s. During that decade only 3,329 Portuguese immigrants arrived in this country; in the ten years that followed the number of immigrants more than doubled as 7,423 of them managed to get to the United States.[208] The first significant change in Portuguese immigration to this country developed out of a natural disaster in the Azores. In 1957 the island of Faial was shaken by the eruption of a new volcano and, although no lives were lost, a considerable amount of damage occurred in one of the more isolated villages and the surrounding area. During the post-World War II years the United States developed a "refugee tradition"; special legislation was enacted time and time again to permit a non-quota flow of immigrants from a particular country into the United States in order that they might escape a difficult situation in their homeland. True to form, Congress enacted the Azorean Refugee Act of 1960. To help ease the problems of resettlement caused by the volcanic eruption, Congress first created 1,500 special non-quota visas to enable heads of family from Faial to immigrate to the United States; in 1960, 2,000 additional non-quota visas were authorized. In all, 4,811 Portuguese immigrated to the United States under the Azorean Refugee Acts.[209]

The Azorean Refugee Acts of 1958 and 1960 marked the beginnings of the third stage of migration from the Azores to the United States. Although immigration under the refugee acts was restricted to people affected by the eruption of the volcano on Faial, the acts were followed in the mid-1960s by a complete revision of the immigration laws of the United States. The National Origin's Legislation of the 1920s was replaced with less restrictive and non-discriminatory quotas. The new law provided:

> the admission of immediate relatives (unmarried children under twenty-one, spouse, and parents of a U.S. citizen) without numerical limitations. It further allows a maximum of 20,000 visas to each Eastern Hemisphere country, preference to be given to unmarried adult sons or daughters of U.S. citizens, then to spouses and unmarried sons or daughters of permanent resident aliens, then to married sons or

[208] *Immigration and Naturalization Service, 1976 Annual Report.* Washington, D.C. 1977. Pp. 86-88.

[209] Francis M. Rogers, "Americans of Portuguese Descent: A Lesson in Differentiation". *Sage Research Paper in the Social Sciences.* Beverly Hills. 1974. P. 33.

daughters of U.S. citizens, then to brothers or sisters of U.S. citizens, and finally to nonpreference immigrants.[210]

The inhabitants of the Azores were in desperate straits by the mid-1960s and welcomed the relief promised by the new immigration laws. António de Oliveira Salazar, the Portuguese chief of state, had ruled that country with an iron hand since 1933 and few benefits reached the Azorean Islands. In addition to the normal, heavy rate of taxation that Portuguese citizens endured, all goods imported to the Azores from a foreign country had to pass through Lisbon first where a special tax was added. Similarly, any product being exported from the islands suffered the same fate. With little say in their local government and only token representation in the national government, the islands were, in every sense of the term, little more than a colony of mainland Portugal. Although they were officially recognized as an integral part of Portugal, they were never treated as such. They were, however, Portuguese citizens and the traditional ties that had evolved over the past four hundred years, partly a result of their proximity to the mainland, firmly identified them as Portuguese. Such was not the case in Angola and Mozambìque — the two major Portuguese colonies in Africa.

While most European colonial powers acknowledged changing world conditions in the post-World War II era and made plans to terminate, as gracefully as possible, the colonial status of their former territories in Africa, Portugal was determined to maintain control over its African colonies. The Portuguese government of António Salazar reacted to African demands for independence by sending more troops to Mozambique, Angola and Portuguese Guinea; the Africans responded with the hit-and-run tactics of guerrilla warfare. For the next fourteen years a colonial war of attrition raged, with varying degrees of intensities, in Portugal's African colonies. Outnumbered almost two to one by its colonists, Portugal was hard pressed to fight a three-front war. Once again the young men of the Azores were faced with conscription into the Portuguese Army. Instead of the prospects of being stationed on the mainland for several years, they now faced the probability of being sent to Africa to fight in a guerrilla war which they could not hope to win. Even Salazar's abdication of power in 1968, a result of poor health, did not end Portugal's involvement in the three-front colonial war; his successor was as committed as Salazar had been to preventing

[210] *Ibid.*

the three African countries from becoming independent nations. As the war continued year after year with no end in sight, immigration to the United States or Canada appealed to more and more young men as an attractive alternative to going off to fight in an unpopular war in Africa. Even parents with young children emigrated to avoid the prospects of future military service for their young sons.[211]

In spite of the number of Azoreans who were able to immigrate to Canada or the United States during the last half of the 1950s, the population of the islands continued to increase and reached a new high of 327,421 individuals in 1960.[212] As the pressure on the limited amount of agricultural land intensified, the dichotomy inherent in the traditional system of land ownership became even more conspicuous. Of the 40,710 agricultural landholdings in the Azores in 1965, 81.8 percent were less than three hectares in size[213] and yet those 81.8 percent controlled only 33.7 percent of all agricultural land (See, Table 8). Their counterparts, the number of holdings in excess of ten hectares, which included only 3.2 percent of all the farms, accounted for 31.8 percent of the total agricultural land. On some islands the contrasts were even more extreme. On São Miguel, for example, 88.3 percent of the farms were concentrated on 46 percent of the agricultural land on the one hand, while on the other, 27.2 percent of the land was controlled by only 2.1 percent of the farms. With only thirty-eight percent of the land even marginally suitable for agriculture and the population still increasing, the prospects of the younger generation being able to acquire enough land to support themselves were very poor.

The possibilties for urban-oriented employment were not any better. With only slightly more than 21,000 inhabitants in 1970, Ponta Delgada, São Miguel, was the largest urban center in the Azores; it was followed by Angra do Heroismo, Terceira with 16,000 and Horta, Faial with 7,000 residents.[214] As district capitals, they were able to provide a limited amount of employment in the various government agencies, but even that was minimal. Lacking an industrial base, and without any prospects of acquiring one, the three urban areas were limited to basic processing and

---

[211] Information is from interviews conducted in the Azores by the author in the summer of 1978.

[212] *10° Recenseamento Geral da Populacão no Continente e Illhas Ajacentes, 1960.* Tomo II. Lisboa. 1960.

[213] A hectare of land is approximately 2.5 acres.

[214] *Acores: Do 25 de Abril ate aos nossos dias.* Lisboa. 1977. P. 143.

TABLE 8
AGRICULTURAL LANDHOLDINGS IN THE AZORES 1965

Islands	Number of Holdings	Area in Farmland (Hectares)	0-3 Hectares (Percent)		3-5 Hectares (Percent)		5-10 Hectares (Percent)		More Than 10 Hectares (Percent)	
			Farms	Area	Farms	Area	Farms	Area	Farms	Area
Santa Maria	1,754	2,857.35	87.0	47.9	7.8	18.4	3.9	16.9	1.3	16.8
São Miguel	17,494	30,854.80	88.3	46.0	6.0	12.9	3.6	13.9	2.1	27.2
Terceira	8,487	18,868.17	80.0	29.8	10.5	18.3	6.8	20.6	2.7	31.3
Graciosa	1,980	2,732.66	88.8	51.1	5.9	16.2	4.2	20.7	1.1	12.0
São Jorge	2,911	10,381.59	68.0	17.6	11.6	12.7	11.9	23.7	8.7	46.0
Pico	4,172	12,239.30	74.5	22.2	9.9	13.0	9.3	21.9	6.3	42.9
Faial	2,428	6,777.80	68.0	28.2	19.4	26.9	9.9	23.8	2.7	21.1
Flores	1,373	4,490.38	72.5	23.2	12.8	15.1	9.0	18.7	5.7	43.0
Corvo	111	375.97	48.7	23.7	31.5	35.4	17.1	32.1	2.7	8.3
TOTAL	40,710	89,578.02	81.8	33.7	8.9	15.6	6.1	18.9	3.2	31.8

Source: *Sumula de Dados Estatisticos*, Departamento Regional de Estudios e Planeamento, (Acores, 1976), p. 21.

packaging of agricultural products and providing goods and services for a poor, rural population. With one exception, the military base on Terceira, non-urban service employment was virtually nonexistent. The air base, which the United States leased from Portugal, provided employment for a number of Azoreans, as support staff for the base and the American servicemen stationed there, but the revenues from leasing the base went to the Portuguese government. Although they welcomed the employment that the installation provided, the natives of Terceira found themselves exposed to conspicuous consumption and forced to compete with the comparatively wealthy American servicemen for housing and other goods and services in the nearby villages. Although the "ugly American" syndrome contributed to a sense of resentment toward American servicemen, it also reinforced the myth that everyone in America was wealthy and helped entice young Azoreans to become immigrants.

Indications that the third wave of migration was in motion first became apparent in the 1960 Census when six of the nine islands registered an absolute decline in population (*See,* Table 9). Even though the other three islands also experienced out-migration after 1950, their net gain was sufficient to account for an overall increase in the archipelago's population between 1950 and 1960. The population of the Azores reached a new high of 327,421 in 1960 with an average density of 368 persons per square mile. Four of the nine islands exceeded 300 persons per square mile; São Miguel and Terceira, with 587 and 473 respectively, were at the top of the list (*See,* Table 9).

The archaic land tenure system, which accentuated the perennial shortage of farm land, limited the ability of the agricultural sector to absorb an increasing population. The developing urban centers were equally unable to provide employment for the expanding labor force and, after 1960, the specter of compulsory military service, to fight a colonial war in Africa, weighed heavily upon the future of the young Portuguese population. With few prospects in their homeland, immigration was, once again, viewed as a viable alternative to a continually deteriorating economic and political situation. Fortunately, both Canada and the United States were receptive to receiving new immigrants in the 1960s and 1970s and many Azoreans took advantage of the opportunity and left the islands to join friends and relatives in America.

The 1970 Census of Portugal recorded a substantial drop in the Azorean population, with every island showing a loss since the

TABLE 9
POPULATION OF THE AZORES 1960-1975

Islands	Pop.[1] 1960	Apparent Change Since 1950	Pop. P/S/M 1960	Pop.[2] 1970	Pop.[3] 1975	Apparent Change Since 1960	Pop. P/S/M 1975
Santa Maria	13,180	+ 1,336	356	9,765	7,784	- 5,396	210
São Miguel	169,170	+ 5,003	587	149,000	136,972	-32,198	475
Terceira	72,479	+12,107	473	65,500	61,450	-11,029	401
Graciosa	8,634	- 883	362	7,180	6,337	- 2,297	264
São Jorge	14,764	- 765	160	12,970	11,930	- 2,834	129
Pico	21,626	- 931	128	18,125	16,096	- 5,530	96
Faial	20,343	- 3,580	308	16,375	14,073	6,270	213
Flores	6,556	- 1,094	119	5,630	5,093	- 1,463	92
Corvo	669	- 59	100	470	355	- 314	53
TOTAL	327,421	+11,134	368	285,015	260,090	-67,331	292

Source: [1] *Recenseamento Geral da População do Continente e ilhas Adjacentes, en 15 de Dezembro 1960.* Tomo II. Instituto Nacional de Estatistica. Lisboa. 1960.

[2] *11° Recenseamento da População Continente e ilhas Adjacentes de 1970.* Instituto Nacional de Estatistica. Lisboa. 1970.

[3] *População dos Açores,* Departamento Regional de Estudios e Planeamento. Açores.

previous census. The apparent loss of 42,406 inhabitants was, in fact, much higher; official emigration records indicate that 75,116 residents departed from the islands between 1960 and 1970.[215] With a natural increase of approximately one percent per year, the population of the Azores was continuing to increase and, if renewed out-migration had not occurred, would have reached 360,000 by 1970. An age-sex pyramid of the 1970 population of the Azores clearly reveals which age group provided the bulk of the new migrants (*See,* Table 10). In 1970, the 20-45 age group accounted for only 14.5 percent of the males and 15.2 percent of the females, for a total of 29.7 percent; in 1950 the same age group contained 18.5 percent of the males and 18.6 percent of the females, or 37.1 percent of the total population. The loss of young adults was also reflected in a decline in the number of births after 1965 and an increase in the proportion of the population over fifty. The impact of the new migration is still primarily apparent in the absence, in the age-sex pyramid, of a substantial proportion of the young adult population; once those new immigrants are firmly established in a new environment, the traditional chain migration can be expected to broaden the affects of the out-migration on the remaining population as parents and siblings are also encouraged to move to the new country.

The tide of Azorean emigrants ebbed and flowed from 1950 to 1976 in direct response to changes in immigration laws in the United States and Canada. During the first three years, before Canada opened its doors to new immigrants, the out-migration averaged only 750 per year; when Canada began accepting immigrants, the yearly average increased to 2,040 between 1953 and 1958. The impact of the Azorean Refugee Acts of 1958 and 1960 were reflected in a temporary increase to 6,800 in 1959 and 1960, afterwards the out-migration declined to 3,500 per year from 1961 until 1965 and most of those went to Canada. The revision in U.S. immigration quotas in 1965 prompted a substantial increase in emigration; during the next ten years the annual flow of departees averaged 10,400.[216] In the twenty-five years prior to 1976, 146,899 Azoreans officially emigrated from their homeland.[217]

In addition, there was a fairly substantial illegal immigration to both the United States and Canada throughout the 1960s and

[215] *Acores: Do 25 de Abril ate aos nossos dias.* P. 144.

[216] Data provided to the author by the Director of the Department of Emigration in Horta, Faial, during the summer of 1978.

[217] *Acores: Do 25 de Abril ate aos nossos dias.* P. 144.

TABLE 10

POPULATION PYRAMID OF THE AZORES—1970

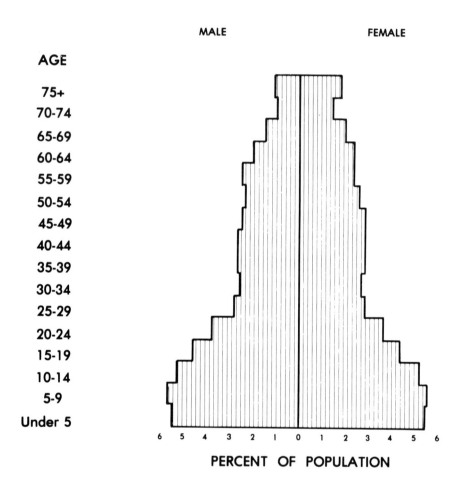

PERCENT OF POPULATION

Source: *XI Recenseamento Geral da Populacao, 1970*
Instituto Nacional de Estatistica, Lisboa, 1970.

1970s. It was not uncommon for Portuguese citizens, and those from other countries as well, to visit the United States or Canada on a tourist visa, find a job through the efforts of friends or relatives, and simply neglect to return to their homeland. The Immigration and Naturalization Service does not check to see that tourists depart, and after several years the illegal immigrant could petition to have his or her status changed to that of a legal alien. Although it required obtaining legal advice, to process the necessary papers, there was seldom any danger of being deported. Illegal immigration enabled the potential emigrants to leave their homeland immediately, once the decision was made to depart, and avoid the delay of waiting one or more years for an opening in the annual quota of legal emigrants. It is impossible to determine precisely how many Portuguese availed themselves of this shortcut, but apparently many did.

Official emigration records indicate that fifty-three percent of the 38,150 emigrants who left the islands in the six-year period 1970-1975 were destined for the United States, while forty-five percent went to Canada. Only two percent of those who made the decision to leave the islands permanently chose a location other than the United States or Canada, which, again, illustrates the continuing influence of social ties in determining where an individual would go once the decision was made to emigrate. Although São Miguel accounted for fifty-two percent of the total Azorean population in 1970, it was the origin of only forty-one percent of the out-migration that occurred between 1970-1975. Of the 15,642 emigrants who left São Miguel during that time, fifty-eight percent were destined for Canada and thirty-nine percent for the United States. With 10,182 departures during the same period, Terceira was the second most important source of emigrants; with twenty-three percent of the Azorean population in 1970, the island contributed twenty-seven percent of the six-year migration total. In contrast to São Miguel, sixty-one percent of those leaving Terceira ended up in the United States while only thirty-seven percent went to Canada. With the exception of Santa Maria and Corvo, where the number leaving were in proportion to each island's share of the Azorean population, and São Miguel, which was noticeably lower, the other six islands were all responsible for a larger share of emigrants leaving the Azores, in the six years, than their respective percentage of the total population in 1970.[218]

Apparently population pressures were perceived, by

---

[218] Data provided to the author by the Director of the Department of Emigration in Horta, Faial, during the summer of 1978.

the inhabitants, as being more severe on the other islands than they were on São Miguel. The fact that Ponta Delgada, the largest urban center in the archipelago, was located on São Miguel and was able to offer a greater number of urban-oriented jobs, may have also contributed to this perception. In addition, between 1970 and 1975 São Miguel lost the equivalent of thirty percent of its 1960 population through emigration; the size and nature of that loss significantly reduced competition for employment among the younger generation of the island. While the incentives to leave were obviously stronger on some islands than on others, the extent of the out-migration, which occurred in a relatively brief time span, was felt throughout the archipelago. A revised population estimate for the Azores in 1975 indicated that the population had declined to 260,090; average density, once again, dropped below 300 persons per square mile. In fifteen years, emigration reduced Santa Maria's population by forty-one percent and lowered the average density on the island from 356 persons per square mile to 210. Faial's population declined by thirty-one percent in that same period while Pico's fell by twenty-six percent. Even Corvo, with its minuscule population of 669 inhabitants in 1960, suffered a forty-seven percent reduction during those fifteen years (See, Table 9).

Preliminary data indicate that the scale of the out-migration declined somewhat after 1975,[219] but the loss of so many inhabitants, even from an over-populated environment, created problems of adjustment. During the summer of 1978 a common complaint heard in the islands was, "It is almost impossible to get dependable agricultural workers", and, "The cost of labor has gone so high that a farmer cannot afford to hire help". The decline in the large surplus population reduced competition for employment and, consequently, increased the cost of labor. One response to increased labor costs was apparent in changing land use patterns; land formerly utilized for producing a variety of foodstuffs was converted to pasture for beef cattle. Large areas, formerly devoted to intensive agriculture, were tranformed into an extensive system of land use, due to increased labor costs, the difficulty in obtaining adequate help, and the existence of a ready market for beef cattle in mainland Portugal. At the same time, to feed their population, the islands were forced to import corn and other foodstuffs, which they had customarily produced.

Other traditional labor intensive activities also suffered from the changing labor market. Handcrafted artifacts, typical of

[219] *Ibid.*

the Azores, became difficult to find and, if available, were frequently produced in the Madeira Islands. Weaving, for local consumption or the occasional tourist, virtually disappeared from the islands. Shore whaling, introduced into the islands by American whalers in the 1850s, was also rapidly disappearing. As late as 1954, it was noted that

> Sperm whaling in these islands is especially interesting because the methods employed are a survival of that old-time whaling generally believed to have quite vanished from the seas. Shore whaling off the coasts of the Azores, prosecuted with the hand harpoon and lance from open boats under oars or sails, is still a considerable industry.[220]

Stepping into an Azorean whaling boat is like taking a step backwards in time. The equipment and techniques employed by these 20th century hunters are identical to those used over one hundred years ago by American whaling vessels. Even the terminology employed in the hunt has been retained and passed on from the earlier whaling period.[221] Although a study of Azorean whaling in the late 1960s found it to still be a viable occupation on the islands of Pico and Faial,[222] by 1978 it was being pursued by a dwindling number of aging, part-time whalers who occupied themselves as longshoremen and farmers while they listened for the sound of the exploding rocket which has traditionally called them to their boats. Whaling, Azorean style, continues to be a hazardous occupation with marginal rewards. As such, it rarely attracts young men who find it much easier and more rewarding to seek their fortunes in a foreign country than in a whale boat. The whaling village of Lajes do Pico, home of one of the few remaining shore whaling crews in the Azores, has, in its own way, felt the impact of out-migration from the islands as sharply as the farmers on São Miguel and the other islands. Like so many other traditional occupations, once common to these islands, whaling is fast disappearing and with it goes the last surviving example of the 19th century whaler.

The current flow of out-migration is sending shock waves throughout Azorean society. With modern transportation, the United

---

[220] Clarke, "Open Boat Whaling in the Azores". P. 283.

[221] Fred Bruemmer, "Survival of American Whaling Terms in the Azores", *American Speech*, 35(1): 20-23. Feb. 1960.

[222] Trevor Housby, *The Hand of God: Whaling in the Azores*. New York. 1971.

States is now only a four-hour flight away from the islands and the flow of traffic between the two countries is substantial. Many emigrants send money to members of their family still living in the Azores and return visits from fairly recent immigrants are not uncommon. Their accounts of jobs and living conditions in the new country continue to stimulate the flow of immigrants, but it is also partially responsible for a growing sense of dissatisfaction with life in the islands. Traditional occupations are falling by the wayside as young people seek alternatives elsewhere and demands for more and improved services, which most see as long overdue, are widespread. The military takeover of the Portuguese government in 1974 brought an end to the disastrous three-front African war, but it has been less successful in dealing with the social, economic and political needs of its citizens both on the mainland and the adjacent islands. Migration continues to be a response to significant differences between one area and another and whether the Azorean populations of the United States and Canada will continue to grow depends, to a large degree, upon how the younger generation perceives the Portuguese government's efforts to introduce social and economic changes into their homeland.

Chapter VII

New Immigrants: The Same but Different

When the final contingent of the second wave of Portuguese migration arrived in the United States during the early 1920s, they found that economic conditions in their new homeland were not as promising as anticipated. The depression that first affected farmers in the late 1920s worsened and became widespread during the 1930s. Although they were not unaccustomed to hard times, most of the Azorean immigrants were inexperienced in surviving in a depressed urban-industrial environment. Hard on the heels of the economic collapse of the 1930s came World War II; while it solved the job shortage and put the nation back to work, it created other pressures, particularly for ethnic minorities. World War II, even more than the previous war, was a war for ideological and political survival; and, as such, it required Herculean efforts on the part of the inhabitants of the United States to supply men and equipment in sufficient quantities to wage a war. In the "us" versus "them" psychology of total warfare, there is little room for the non-committed; under the guise of patriotism many former immigrants abandoned their native tongue, anglicized their name, and de-emphasized "un-American" cultural traditions. The pressure to be a "100 percent American" during the war years was most pronounced in urban settings where there was greater day-to-day contact between immigrants and nonimmigrants; the isolation of rural life tended to diffuse the impact of many immediate, short-term side effects of the war effort.

Without any substantial input from new immigrants, cultural reinforcement lessened with each passing year. Only 3,329 Portuguese immigrants entered the United States between 1931 and 1940, which was fewer than 350 per year; although the total for the next decade doubled

(7,423), it still averaged less than 750 per year. The minimal cultural impact of 10,722 new immigrants in twenty years is even more apparent when compared to the base population of 278,726 inhabitants of Portuguese foreign stock residing in the United States in 1930. Economic and social pressures combined to force conformity toward some preconceived model of an American citizen and the absence of any large scale immigration of people exemplifying traditional cultural values of the Azores greatly facilitated the dual process of acculturation and assimilation.

Economic conditions continued to improve in the United States during the 1950s and, at the same time, worsened in the Azores, thereby creating significant differences between the two areas and pressure for the current stage of migration. The volcanic eruptions on Faial in 1957, which motivated the Azorean Refugee Acts of 1958 and 1960, also aroused a great deal of sympathy from Portuguese Americans for their relatives in the islands. Although the social network had suffered from reduced contact between inhabitants of the islands and the United States during the thirty-year interlude, it still effectively connected the two populations. As it had for previous immigrants, the social network came to the aid of refugees from the natural disaster on Faial and assisted them in securing employment and housing.

The Portuguese immigrants of the 1960s and 1970s were motivated by the same forces that compelled their compatriots to depart the Azores throughout the previous one hundred fifty years; namely, a change to improve themselves economically. The everpresent specter of overpopulation and military conscription for the males, as always, were contributing factors. Little has changed in the daily life of Azoreans during the previous century and a half. Immigrants now make the trip from the islands to the United States by jet but, for the majority, the four-hour flight is their first experience in an airplane. Two characteristics of these new immigrants, however, do distinguish them from the earlier groups: education and a sense of nationality. Overall, they tend to be better educated than previous Portuguese immigrants; for most the change is minimal, an elementary education for them versus no education for their grandparents and many of their parents. While their forefathers frequently thought of themselves as being from a particular village or island first, followed by the Azores and, lastly, as Portuguese, the perspective is almost the reverse now. A sense of being Portuguese permeates these newcomers; granted, they are Azoreans from Pico, Faial, São Miguel or one of the other six islands, but they are Portuguese first. This sense of nationalism is a fairly recent phenomenon and is a result, in part, of the nature of the prolonged colonial wars in Africa and the Portuguese government's efforts to generate patriotic support for an unpopular war.

In the last fifteen years, almost as many immigrants have come to the United States as arrived during the thirty years from 1890-1920, when worldwide immigration was at its peak. The extensive social network between Portuguese in the United States and the Azores, which facilitated the migration by finding jobs and housing for newcomers, encouraged a high degree of concentration of Portuguese immigrants in a relatively small number of communities. Large concentrations of immigrants, all in need of jobs, housing and other assistance, arrived in such a short period of time that they were inevitably a disrupting force, even if only temporarily. The enormous task of spatially and temporally accommodating the influx of new immigrants created adjustment problems for both immigrants and Portuguese Americans.

Although the same single-minded attention to achieving economic well-being was as characteristic of past generations of immigrants as it is the current generation, it is now cause for disdain on the part of many Portuguese Americans and non-Portuguese. In the generation between the second and third stage of Portuguese migration major social legislation was enacted to provide at least minimal economic security for the working population and the elderly in this country. And, in spite of the current concern about how to continue financing that legislation, it did generate major social changes. Children of immigrants, who themselves grew up in America, sometimes cannot fully appreciate the true nature of the social and economic system left behind by their parents and, now, by the new immigrants arriving from the Azores. Never having lived under such a system, nor having experienced the emotional impact of being an immigrant, second generation Portuguese Americans frequently cannot comprehend the immigrants' overriding concern with economic security. Most people have to go into debt to emigrate and the level of indebtedness usually increases while they are getting established in their new home. Before they can even start to think about achieving the economic security which motivated them to migrate in the first place, they have to turn their full attention to retiring those family debts. Usually, "every able-bodied member of a family contributes to its income and welfare".[223]

---

[223] Marilyn A. Trueblood, "The Melting Pot and Ethnic Revitalization". In *Ethnic Encounters: Identities and Contexts*. Edited by G.L. Hicks and P.E. Leis. (North Scituate, Mass., 1977, P.

While they genuinely want to see these new immigrants succeed, many Portuguese Americans resent the plethora of government programs which, although designed to help immigrants adjust to their new environment, seem to favor immigrants over native born Americans. As one second generation Portuguese American expressed it,

> Sure! We came when you didn't have all this and that free money for immigrants and minorities. We had to work for everything we got. Nobody gave us anything for nothing. Now these people are coming in and get bussed to special bilingual schools—so they don't learn English and are proud of it! They get free lunches, they get paid to go to school, they get everything free we had to work for. They buy 10 houses where we're lucky if we own one with the mortgage paid. And then you tell us we should be like *them*—pushy, grabby, and not even trying to be American! That's the thanks we get for working hard and keeping things right.[224]

Whatever the reaction to the sometimes over-zealous efforts of the new immigrants, which frequently get then stereotyped as "materialistic greenhorns", the current wave of immigration has prompted many Portuguese Americans to reconsider their cultural heritage. Whether it stems from a desire to counter the image of Portugal and Portuguese that the new immigrants are creating, or from a need to identify themselves as Portuguese as a means of distinguishing themselves from other ethnic groups, Portuguese communities in the United States are experiencing an ethnic revitalization movement. Such movements are most noticeable in the urban areas, such as Fall River, New Bedford, Providence and San Leandro, where many of these new immigrants are experiencing an ethnic revitalization movement. Such movements are concentrated. One of the most glaring inconsistencies in the current ethnic revitalization movement, however, is the attempt to identify with a classical, elitist culture characteritic of mainland Portugal, which was far removed from the peasant society of the Azores from which most Portuguese American immigrants originated.[225].

---

162. *Also see,* June Namias, "Antonio Cardoso—Boy from the Azores". In *First Generation: In the Words of Twentieth-Century American Immigrants.* Boston. 1978. Pp. 171-75.

[224] Estellie M. Smith, "Estão Aqui Mesmo". Unpublished paper, P. 11.

[225] Trueblood, "The Melting Pot and Ethnic Revitalization", P. 165

As the Census of 1960 revealed, the continuing trickle of immigration and the first group of refugees were almost sufficient to maintain the population of Portuguese foreign stock in the United States at the 1930 level. The census enumerated 277,402 residents with a Portuguese heritage in 1960, which was a drop of only 1,324 from the 1930 count (*See,* Table 11). Nationwide the distribution was a continuation of earlier patterns; three states (California, Massachusetts, and Rhode Island) still accounted for eighty percent of the Portuguese foreign stock. An additional four states (Connecticut, Hawaii, New York, and New Jersey), none with as much as five percent, brought the combined total to 94.3 percent. Although Hawaii's Portuguese population continued its downward spiral, Connecticut, New York, and New Jersey all experienced noticeable growth.

The pre-1960 growth in the Portuguese population located along the east coast of the United States was a harbinger of things to come in the 1960s and 1970s. The revision of U.S. immigration laws could not have come at a more opportune time for the severely overpopulated Azores and the inhabitants reacted by departing their homeland by the tens of thousands. The annual average of new Portuguese immigrants arriving during the 1960s was higher than the total for the entire decade of the 1940s. In the twenty years prior to 1950 only 10,752 Portuguese immigrated to the United States; in the eighteen years between 1961 and 1977 more than 150,000 came to this country—thirty-five percent of the total Portuguese immigration since 1820 (*See,* Table 12). In the nine years from 1968 through 1976 an average of 12,042 new immigrants arrived each year and there was a noticeable shift in their destination; the concentration on the east coast became even greater than it had traditionally been.[226]

A new wave of immigration has been entering the United States since the mid-1960s, but reliable information on the current distribution of Portuguese immigrants, and other immigrant groups as well, is difficult to obtain. Although the Census of 1970 collected information on ethnic origin of the United States' population, it was never published. To make matters worse, the 1980 Census also has not gathered comparable information on national origin. However, the Immigration and Naturalization Service does require all legal aliens to register at the beginning of each year and, in 1978, 122,330 permanent resident Portuguese aliens registered in the United States (*See,* Table 11). In addition to those 122,330 Portuguese

---

[226] *Immigration and Naturalization Service, Annual Report,* various years from 1966 to 1976.

TABLE 11
PORTUGUESE POPULATION OF THE UNITED STATES
1870-1978

Political Unit	1870 Number	1870 %	1900 Number	1900 %	1930* Number	1930* %	1960*[1] Number	1960*[1] %	1978**[2] Number	1978**[2] %
California	3,435	40.0	15,583	32.4	99,194	35.6	97,489	35.1	21,261	17.4
Connecticut	221	2.6	655	1.4	4,701	1.7	9,930	3.6	8,737	7.1
Hawaii	—	—	7,668	15.9	19,121	6.8	9,325	3.4	117	0.1
Illinois	856	9.9	—	—	—	—	—	—	—	—
Massachusetts	2,555	29.7	17,885	37.2	105,076	37.7	95,328	34.4	46,792	38.3
New Jersey	—	—	62	0.3	5,099	1.8	8,933	3.2	16,487	13.5
New York	334	3.9	823	1.7	7,758	2.8	11,497	4.1	7,455	6.1
Rhode Island	189	2.2	2,865	5.9	29,097	10.4	29,155	10.5	16,351	13.4
All Others	1,015	11.7	2,558	5.2	8,680	3.2	15,745	5.7	5,247	4.2
TOTAL	8,605	100.0	48,099	100.0	278,726	100.0	277,402	100.0	122,330	100.0

* Foreign White Stock. Includes foreign born Portuguese and their children—the first and second generation.

** Permanent Resident Aliens.

[1] *Census of the Population, 1960* Vol. 1, *Characteristics of the Population.* Part 1 *United States Summary.*

[2] Data furnished by Immigration and Naturalization Service, Washington, D.C.

TABLE 12

PORTUGUESE IMMIGRATION TO THE UNITED STATES
1820-1977

Time	Number	Percent of Total
1820-1870	5,272	1.2
1871-1880	14,082	3.2
1881-1890	16,978	3.9
1891-1900	27,508	6.3
1901-1910	69,149	15.9
1911-1920	89,732	20.7
1921-1930	29,994	6.9
1820-1930	252,715	58.1
1931-1940	3,329	0.8
1941-1950	7,423	1.7
1951-1960	19,588	4.5
1961-1970	76,065	17.5
1971-1977	75,397	17.4
1931-1977	181,802	41.9
TOTAL	434,517	100.0%

Source: *Immigration and Naturalization Service, 1976 Annual Report.* Pp.
86-88. 1977 Data from correspondence with Immigration and Naturalization
Service, Washington, D.C.

classified as permanent resident aliens in 1978, another 26,129 became
naturalized citizens between 1966 and 1976.

Although the data collected by the Immigration and
Naturalization Service is not quite so precise as that collected by the Census
Bureau, since aliens are recorded by ZIP code areas—which frequently do

not correspond exactly with county boundaries, they do indicate the overall distribution of Portuguese aliens and provide a basis for comparison. Based on that data, the degree of concentration in 1978 was even greater than in 1960; in 1978 six states contained 95.8 percent of the permanent resident Portuguese aliens and, although there was a noticeable shift to the east coast of the United States, the new immigrants were concentrated in the same states in 1978 as the Portuguese population was from 1900 to 1960. The most noticeable difference in the distribution of Portuguese aliens in 1978 and the Portuguese foreign stock in 1960 occurred in California where only 17.4 percent of the former were located versus 35.1 percent of the latter. The most substantial increase was reported for New Jersey, with 13.5 percent of the Portuguese aliens in 1978 but only 3.2 percent of the 1960 Portuguese population (*See,* Table 11).

Massachusetts furnishes an excellent example of a state that has experienced rapid growth in its Portuguese immigrant community in the last fifteen years. The Portuguese foreign stock in Massachusetts in 1960, 95,324 individuals, was concentrated in the same six counties where the 1930 population of 105,076 was located. In spite of the approximate ten percent decline in the Portuguese population during those thirty years, there was only a slight decline in the percentage of concentration in those six countries—from 95 percent to 93.1 percent (*See,* Map 7). In 1960 there were 11,420 Portuguese aliens living in the state; by 1978 the number had increased four-fold and the state was home to 46,792 permanent resident Portuguese aliens.[227] In addition to the 46,792 permanent resident Portuguese aliens still living in the state in 1978, more than 10,000 other Portuguese immigrants became naturalized citizens during that same period.[228]

Five of the six counties where the Portuguese have been concentrated in Massachusetts since 1900 still accounted for ninety percent of the 46,792 permanent resident aliens in 1978. Barnstable County, where traditionally the Portuguese have turned to fishing as an occupation, was not selected as a destination by many new immigrants. In its place was Hampshire County, in the western portion of the state, with 4.3 percent of the new immigrants, and Norfolk County, with 3.2 percent. Bristol County, with 58.7 percent of the Portuguese aliens, was still the most favored destination even though it suffered from high unemployment rates and was

---

[227] *Ibid.* Various years from 1960-1976. Data for 1977-78 furnished by Immigration and Naturalization Service, Washington, D.C.

[228] *Ibid.*

considered an economically depressed area.[229] The war effort of the 1940s provided a temporary reprieve for the depressed textile industry of Massachusetts and neighboring states, but the prosperity was short lived. The obsolete factories were unable to compete successfully in the economy of the 1950s and 1960s. And, as they closed down, unemployment became a serious problem in the former textile centers. The lack of jobs for long time residents of Bristol County was compounded by competition from large numbers of unskilled Portuguese immigrants who arrived in the late 1960s and throughout the 1970s and their arrival aggravated tensions in the already severely depressed communities where they concentrated. A noticeable shift toward the larger urban centers, where employment opportunities for unskilled workers were apparently more abundant, was another characteristic of this new stage of migration. Boston, for example, located in Suffolk County, contained the second-highest concentration of permanent resident Portuguese aliens in Massachusetts in 1978—some 15.5 percent of the state's total (*See,* Map 7).

There was little noticeable change in either the size or distribution of the Portuguese population in Rhode Island between 1930 and 1960. Each census found slightly more than 29,000 Portuguese foreign stock living in the state with ninety-nine percent of them located in the same four counties. The current wave of migration increased the size of Rhode Island's Portuguese population by approximately forty percent. In addition to the 16,351 permanent resident Portuguese aliens residing in the state in 1978, another 2,500 had become naturalized citizens since 1966. [230] In 1978, Rhode Island's share of the nation's total of new Portuguese immigrants increased to 13.4 percent and was accompanied by a decided shift away from the rural areas and toward the urbanized area of Providence. Newport County, which had 19.1 percent of the state's Portuguese population in 1960, only accounted for 1.1 percent of the new immigrants in 1978 while Providence County, with 54.9 percent in 1960, contained 75.1 percent of the permanent resident Portuguese aliens in 1978 (*See,* Map 8).

The Portuguese population of Connecticut doubled between 1930 and 1960 and, while they continued to be concentrated in four counties, the relative degree of concentration followed the direction of change which first occurred between 1900 and 1930. The percentage of Portuguese living in New London County, the old whaling center, steadily

---

[229] Wolforth, *The Portuguese in America, P. 61.*

[230] *Immigration and Naturalization Service, Annual Report,* various years from 1966-1976.

MAP 7

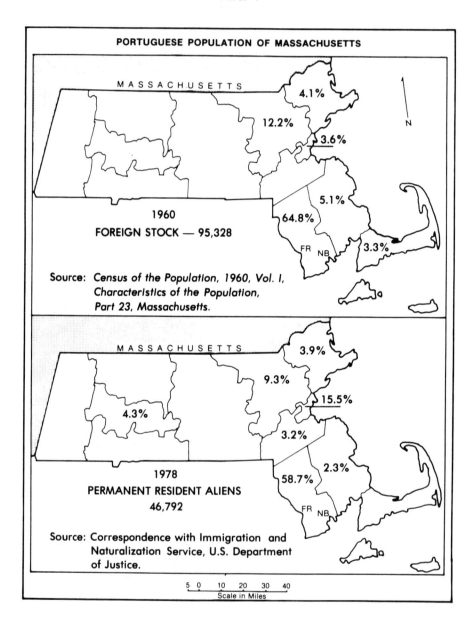

PORTUGUESE POPULATION OF MASSACHUSETTS

MASSACHUSETTS

4.1%

12.2%

3.6%

5.1%

64.8%

FR NB

3.3%

1960
FOREIGN STOCK — 95,328

Source: Census of the Population, 1960, Vol. I,
Characteristics of the Population,
Part 23, Massachusetts.

MASSACHUSETTS

3.9%

9.3%

15.5%

4.3%

3.2%

58.7%

2.3%

FR NB

1978
PERMANENT RESIDENT ALIENS
46,792

Source: Correspondence with Immigration and
Naturalization Service, U.S. Department
of Justice.

5 0   10   20   30   40
Scale in Miles

MAP 8

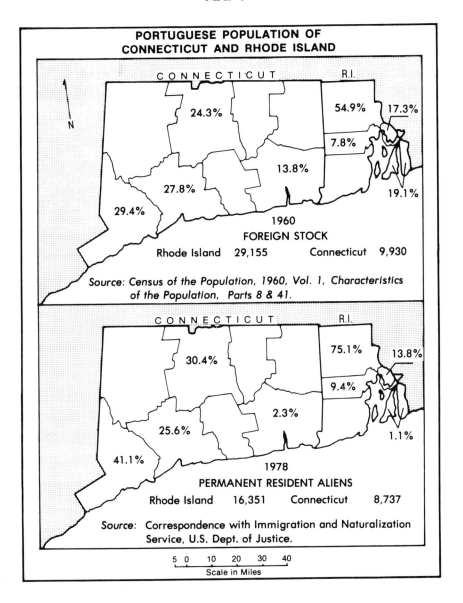

**PORTUGUESE POPULATION OF
CONNECTICUT AND RHODE ISLAND**

CONNECTICUT   R.I.

24.3%   54.9%   17.3%

7.8%

13.8%

27.8%

29.4%   19.1%

1960
FOREIGN STOCK

Rhode Island   29,155   Connecticut   9,930

Source: Census of the Population, 1960, Vol. 1, Characteristics
of the Population, Parts 8 & 41.

CONNECTICUT   R.I.

75.1%   13.8%

30.4%

9.4%

2.3%

25.6%
                               1.1%

41.1%

1978
PERMANENT RESIDENT ALIENS

Rhode Island   16,351   Connecticut   8,737

Source: Correspondence with Immigration and Naturalization
Service, U.S. Dept. of Justice.

5 0   10   20   30   40
Scale in Miles

declined as the other three counties increased. Although the Portuguese population of Connecticut was still relatively small in 1960, it increased almost sixty percent by 1978 and the shift away from New London County was even more severe by 1978 when only 2.3 percent of the Portuguese aliens registered as living in that county. Fairfield County, the closest of the four to New York City, experienced the most significant increase in Portuguese population in the state; 41.1 percent of the new immigrants were located there (*See,* Map 8).

The West Coast experience was quite different from what transpired on the opposite side of the continent but the change was not obvious until after 1960. The total Portuguese population of California declined only slightly between 1930 and 1960 and the only noticeable change in the relative distribution of that population appeared in the southern part of the state. Both Los Angeles and San Diego counties had less than two percent of the Portuguese population in 1930; by 1960, however, the former was home to 5.2 percent of the Portuguese in California and the latter accounted for 3.5 percent. The major concentrations continued to be in the San Francisco Bay Area and the Central Valley (*See,* Map 9).

By the 1960s, Portuguese Americans living in California were, for the most part, "solidly 'middle' in status as well as class".[231] Declining interest in their cultural heritage frequently accompanied Portuguese urban middle class status. The Portuguese celebration in San Diego, for example, died out in 1963 after being an annual event for more than fifty years. As one of its lifelong sponsors lamented: "Nobody wants to work on the festas anymore, we learned. The young people don't care. The old ones are dying out, getting too old for the responsibility."[232] In contrast to the east coast, California did not attract its normal share of new Portuguese immigrants arriving after 1965 and, consequently, Portuguese communities suffered from a lack of cultural revitalization.

Two major changes were apparent in the Portuguese population of California in 1978; the first was a significant decline in the state's share of permanent resident aliens and the second was an increase in the percentage living in the urbanized areas of the state. With 21,261 Portuguese aliens in 1978, California accounted for only 17.4 percent of the new immigrants, which was the first time since the days of the Gold Rush

---

[231] Leder, "Cultural Persistence in a Portuguese American Community", P. 57.

[232] Oliver, *Never Backward,* P. 148.

MAP 9

PORTUGUESE POPULATION OF CALIFORNIA

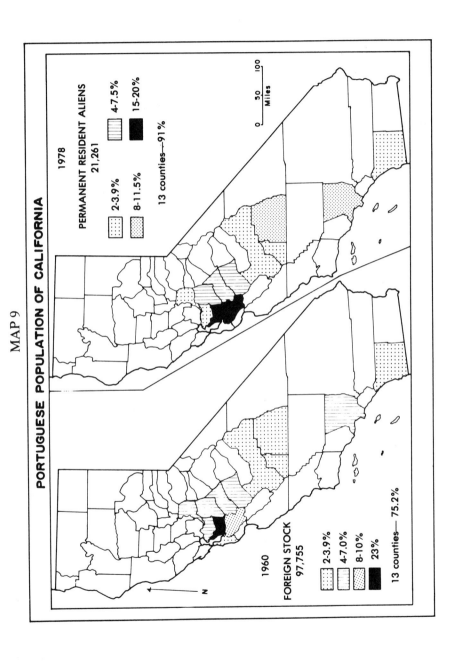

1978

PERMANENT RESIDENT ALIENS
21,261

2-3.9%   4-7.5%

8-11.5%   15-20%

13 counties—91%

0   50   100
Miles

1960

FOREIGN STOCK
97,755

2-3.9%

4-7.0%

8-10%

23%

13 counties— 75.2%

N

that California was home to less than thirty percent of the nation's total Portuguese population. While the number of new Portuguese immigrants residing in Massachusetts quadrupled between 1965 and 1978, in California it only doubled.[233] Diminishing economic opportunities for Portuguese immigrants in traditional California occupations was most likely at the root of the decline. On the east coast most new immigrants ended up as factory workers after 1890, while agriculture was the main attraction in California. With the changing nature of agriculture throughout the United States, particularly in the degree of mechanization, the increase in the size of the farms and, most importantly, the amount of capital required to enter farming, it was much more difficult for an immigrant to get started in farming in the 1970s than it had previously been. The small family farm is no longer a viable economic enterprise in California, and the would-be farmer is now faced with the choice of getting bigger or getting out. Unwilling or unable to remain on the farms where they were raised, many second and third generation Portuguese Americans joined the ranks of urban America during the 1960s and 1970s. In the 1970s, the likelihood that an immigrant could find a job in the factories on the east coast was much greater than the prospect of eventually becoming an independent farmer in California.

The distribution of Portuguese immigrants within California in 1978 also favored urban over rural areas. The percentage of new immigrants increased in both Los Angeles and San Francisco between 1960 and 1978; Los Angeles County's share increased from 5.2 percent in 1960 to 11.5 percent in 1978, while San Francisco went from 2.4 percent to 5.3 percent during that time. Although the data from ZIP codes is not absolutely precise when converted to county boundaries, the concentration of Portuguese in the three major bay area counties appears to have remained almost the same. In 1960, Alameda, Santa Clara, and Contra Costa Counties represented thirty-eight percent of the Portuguese population of the state; in 1978 the same three counties contained thirty-six percent of the permanent resident Portuguese aliens. Tulare County, the center of Portuguese dairy farming in the San Joaquin Valley was the only agricultural county to show a substantial increase in the percentage of Portuguese between 1960 and 1978; it went from 3.3 percent to 8.1 percent (*See,* Map 9).

Distance and discrimination have combined to limit the Hawaiian Islands' attractiveness as a destination for Portuguese im-

---

[233] *Immigration and Naturalization Service, Annual Report,* various years from 1966-1976. Data for 1977 and 1978 furnished by INS, Washington, D.C.

migrants since the first importation of Portuguese families as contract laborers in 1878. The technology of modern transportation has greatly reduced the time involved in getting from the Azores to the Hawaiian Islands, but at a substantial increase in price. One indication that the Portuguese American population of Hawaii has finally overcome the economic liabilities that caused them to be discriminated against by the ruling caucasian class, was the emergence of a Portuguese cultural revival in the mid-1950s. One hundred years after they first began to immigrate to the Hawaiian Islands, there are indications that

> many of Hawaii's Portuguese have become confi-
> dent enough of their social and economic status to
> proceed beyond assimilation and to begin a search
> for their identity as a distinct and valued cultural
> group.[234]

Between 1930 and 1960 the Portuguese foreign stock in Hawaii declined from 15,408 to 9,325 and continued to shift away from the agricultural islands and to the urban area of Honolulu. By 1960, 60.4 percent of the Portuguese population of Hawaii was located in Honolulu County. The best indicator that Portuguese immigrants no longer perceived the Hawaiian Islands as a desirable place to live, in spite of improvements in transportation and a reduction in discrimination, is illustrated by the number of new immigrants that went there after 1960. In 1978, when more than 122,000 Portuguese were registered as permanent resident aliens in the United States, only 117 of them, less than 0.1 percent, were to be found in the Hawaiian Islands (*See,* Map 10).

The largest concentration of Portuguese Americans in the United States, employment opportunities and the ease of accessibility from the Azores at a relatively low price, are attracting the vast majority of new Portuguese immigrants to the eastern seaboard. Seventy-eight percent of all the permanent resident Portuguese aliens in the United States were located in the five states of Massachusetts, Rhode Island, Connecticut, New York, and New Jersey in 1978.[235] Many of the former textile workers in Massachusetts, who were forced to leave that state when the textile industry collapsed in the 1920s and 1930s, settled in Newark, New Jersey, and found employment in the garment industry and other low-paying, non-skilled

---

[234] John Henry Felix and Peter F. Senecal, *The Portuguese in Hawaii*. Honolulu. 1978. P. 119.

[235] Data furnished by INS, Washington, D.C.

MAP 10

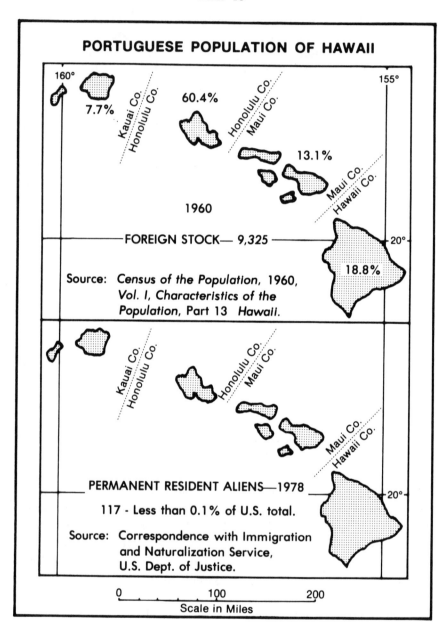

PORTUGUESE POPULATION OF HAWAII

160°

7.7%

Kauai Co.
Honolulu Co.

60.4%

Honolulu Co.
Maui Co.

155°

13.1%

Maui Co.
Hawaii Co.

1960

20°

—————— FOREIGN STOCK— 9,325 ——————

18.8%

Source: *Census of the Population, 1960,*
Vol. I, Characteristics of the
Population, Part 13 Hawaii.

Kauai Co.
Honolulu Co.

Honolulu Co.
Maui Co.

Maui Co.
Hawaii Co.

PERMANENT RESIDENT ALIENS—1978

20°

117 - Less than 0.1% of U.S. total.

Source: Correspondence with Immigration
and Naturalization Service,
U.S. Dept. of Justice.

0   100   200

Scale in Miles

industries. These Portuguese immigrants, who were, for the most part, recent arrivals, formed the nucleus of a Portuguese community in New Jersey. As recent newcomers, their social ties with friends and relatives still living in the Azores were very strong. When immigration restrictions were modified, first by the Azorean Refugee Acts and later by the revision of the basic immigration law in 1965, these former immigrants, now living in New Jersey, encouraged friends and relatives to join them. By 1978, with 12,078 permanent resident Portuguese aliens, Essex County, New Jersey, housed the third largest concentration of new Portuguese immigrants on the east coast; it was exceeded only by Bristol County, Massachusetts, and Providence, Rhode Island.[236]

Two major trends are apparent in the settlement patterns of new Portuguese immigrants who have arrived in the United States since the revision of immigration restrictions: there is a decided urban focus to the new settlement patterns and a new core area of settlement is being created. One of the most obvious characteristics of the new migration, both on the east and west coast, is the inability of rural areas to attract new immigrants. Granted, the U.S. is an urban society, but the most persistent preservers of their Azorean cultural heritage have been those Portuguese living in rural areas. Whether the scale of the current migration will be sufficiently large to overcome the cultural disadvantages of urban life, and thereby maintain an interest in the Portuguese ethnic heritage, remains to be seen. An overall analysis of settlement patterns of new Portuguese immigrants in the five-state area of the east coast also reveals a new core of settlement around the periphery of New York City. Slightly more than twenty-five percent of the new Portuguese immigrants on the east coast of the United States were concentrated in a six-county area surrounding New York City in 1978; those counties were: Fairfield, Conn.; Westchester, N.Y.; Essex and Union, N.J.; and Queens and Nassau, N.Y.[237] (See, Map 11). Although each of these counties has had a small Portuguese population since the end of the second stage of migration, the rapidity of current growth in those counties indicates that a new Portuguese settlement core is firmly established on the east coast.

The emergence of a new core area of settlement illustrates, once again, the effectiveness of the social networks between Portuguese living in the United States and those remaining in the Azores.

[236] *Ibid.*

[237] *Ibid.*

MAP 11

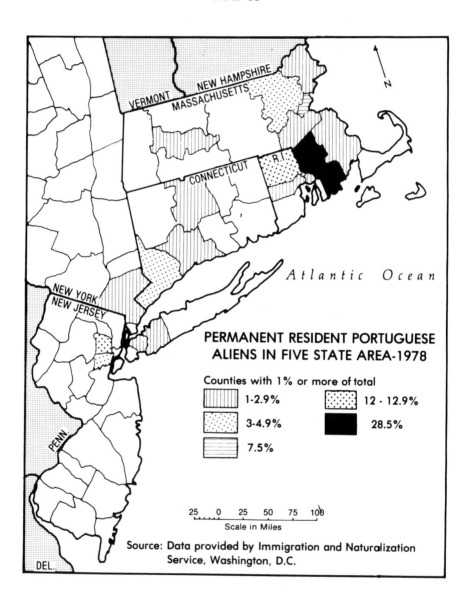

PERMANENT RESIDENT PORTUGUESE
ALIENS IN FIVE STATE AREA-1978

Counties with 1% or more of total

1-2.9%   12 - 12.9%

3-4.9%   28.5%

7.5%

25   0   25   50   75   100
Scale in Miles

Source: Data provided by Immigration and Naturalization
Service, Washington, D.C.

They continue to influence settlement patterns and provide employment opportunities for the new immigrants, even though economic conditions have changed radically since the 1920s when the second stage of migration was abruptly terminated. Neither agriculture in California nor textile mills in Massachusetts offer employment opportunities in sufficient numbers to accommodate the new influx of immigrants. There are still jobs, however, even for the unskilled, non-industrial immigrants from the Azores and particularly for those who are willing to take service jobs or industrial work at the lower entry levels. The urban focus of the current migration, with its emphasis on large urban centers such as Los Angeles, the San Fransisco Bay Area, Toronto, Boston, Providence, and, increasingly, New York City, indicates that the new arrivals are both aware that the greatest availability of such jobs tends to be in or on the periphery of the larger urban centers and quite willing to accept living in a large urban environment to have the opportunity to find what they seek most as immigrants—a chance to improve life materially for themselves and their families.

Chapter VIII

Yesterday, Today and Tomorrow: The Portuguese Presence in America

Migration has traditionally been perceived as a solution for mankind's problems. When, for one reason or another, conditions have become unbearable in a particular location and appeared to be significantly better in another, the human reaction has been to leave the one for the other. In that sense, human migration is timeless; it is, in truth, a story without an end. The characters change, from generation to generation, depending upon the specific motivations for a particular migration and the availability of a viable alternative, but the plot remains basically the same—an attempt to improve the political, economic or social well-being of a people by moving to a new location. In many ways, then, migration is a non-confrontation solution to human problems; in spite of the trauma of dislocation and personal adjustment, for some, migration is preferable to trying to bring about change within the native setting. Change, however, is one of the invariable consequences of migration. Conditions are modified in the homeland, in a variety of ways, by the departure of large numbers of the population; similarly, there is a discernible impact on their chosen destination as a new population, accompanied by their traditions and cultural values, adjusts to and modifies their new location. Sometimes these changes are readily observable; other times one has to look more intently to fully appreciate the impact of a particular migration.

Within the Azores few substantive changes have occurred in the past century and a half. Agriculture, the basis of the economy, is still constricted by an archaic system of land tenure which keeps control of most of the best land in the hands of a small minority who, frequently, are absentee landlords. The Portuguese political system, still in the throes of trying to establish a democratic system of government, has yet to stabilize sufficiently to govern the country effectively. The fifty-year dictatorship of the Salazar government replaced an earlier monarchy and was, in turn, finally overthrown by a disillusioned military which is now trying to create a democratic system of government. Democracy is proving to be a heady experience for a population accustomed to a dictatorship; with so many wrongs needing to be righted and every institution crying out for reform or reorganization, the new political system has been unable to satisfy anyone. In the past five years the country has experienced no fewer than ten government upheavals and is yet to forge an effective governing coalition out of the various political parties.[238]. While the political system drifts about in search of goals and a means of achieving them, economic stagnation and social upheavals compound the political chaos. With so many problems close at hand for the Portuguese government, it is not surprising that the Azores continue to be neglected and somewhat isolated from the turmoil of change sweeping the mainland.

The most notable changes apparent in the islands today are in education, electrification, and the depopulating effects of the current migration. A concerted effort on the part of the Portuguese government to make at least elementary education available to all inhabitants is substantially reducing the rate of illiteracy which historically has been widespread throughout Portugal. In addition to reducing illiteracy, the government is working to bring electricity to every village in the islands; yet the full impact of the current energy crisis and skyrocketing fuel prices on the electrification program remains to be seen. Electricity is, however, invariably accompanied by the ubiquitous television which, in its own way, is accelerating the process of change in the Azores. Nothing, however, has had an impact comparable to the departure of approximately 150,000 Azoreans during the past twenty years. Such a reduction in population creates social and economic repercussions which are both beneficial and detrimental. Government programs, such as the drive to eliminate illiteracy, are easier to accomplish with fewer people, but the transition from labor surplus to a labor short economy creates problems of a different nature. The labor shortage is most apparent in its effects on agriculture where it is causing widespread changes in land use practices and a drop in the production of foodstuffs. Though absent, many recent immigrants send money to assist their parents and family members still living in the islands and, in that way,

---

[238] Norman Sklarewitz, "Portugal: Slow Going Toward Strong Democracy", *The Christian Science Monitor,* March 20, 1979, P.9.

continue to contribute to the local economy. The foreign currency they send to the Azores is sorely needed by the Portuguese govenment.

In an effort to stimulate non-industrial economic development, the Portuguese government has sought to attract international tourism to the country. Expanding the tourist trade would provide additional employment in service occupations and it is a clean, non-polluting industry. Without a well developed infrastructure of hotels and transportation facilities, however, even the potential for effectively promoting a tourist industry to capitalize on the picturesque Azorean setting remains largely unexploited. At present, adequate tourist accommodations are only available in the three urban centers and transportation continues to be a major bottleneck. The larger airplanes used on international routes are restricted by their size to landing on either Santa Maria or Terceira, while Faial and São Miguel have the only other airports on the islands. Transportation between the other five islands is dependent upon the weather and infrequent inter-island boat connections. In addition, tourism has at least one other serious drawback: many of the luxury goods associated with tourism today have to be imported from other countries, which reduces the net economic benefit to Portugal.

Former immigrants and the children of immigrants constitute most of the Azorean tourist trade that originates in the United States. The scale of the present migration is such that virtually everyone in the islands has a relative or close friend who has recently migrated to the United States or Canada and there is a great deal of interaction between these recent immigrants and their homeland. The historical pattern of migration, together with the current trend, have combined to create a natural affinity for the United States where so many former inhabitants of the Azores are now living. One manifestation of that feeling was apparent in a half-hearted effort during the 1970s to promote separation of the Azores from Portugal and some type of unification with the United States. While such talk remains wishful thinking on the part of its proponents, they reason that at least the United States recognizes the strategic value of their location, as witnessed by the U.S. air base on Terceira, and the inhabitants of the islands do have more family connections in the United States than on mainland Portugal. The same reaction to neglect from the mainland also appeared at the height of the second stage of migration (1902) when the idea of separation from Portugal and annexation to the United States was first advanced.[239] Although unification with the United States is not seriously

---

[239] Josef Berger, *In Great Waters*, P. 263.

being considered by anyone, there is a strong desire for Azorean autonomy on the part of the inhabitants of the islands; but there is considerable divergence of opinion as to the form such autonomy should take. Some see it as complete independence for the islands, others favor political autonomy with a separate Azorean government ruling the islands. Unable to agree on what autonomy should mean, it is unlikely that it will make any meaningful difference for everyday life in the Azores.

While the symbiotic relationship between the United States and the Azores continues to function, with Azoreans providing unskilled labor for the U.S. economy and the United States serving as an escape valve for the overpopulated islands, the nature of that relationship is constantly changing. The New England whalers relied heavily upon Azorean peasants for their crews from 1840 through the 1880s and, in the process, transported thousands of young men from their homeland to the developing United States where they found employment in the fishing fleets of New England and the farms of California. Settlement patterns in the initial stage of Portuguese migration to the United States, which were concentrated on the east and west coasts, clearly reflected the influence of whaling, both in transporting the immigrants and providing early locational nodes for settlement, and the attraction of the California Gold Rush. Most of those early immigrants departed from a rural environment in the islands and located in rural areas or small towns in the United States.

Portuguese immigration continued to be concentrated in a few states during the second stage of migration, but a considerable difference developed between the east and west coasts in occupational opportunities and subsequent location patterns. Industrializing New England needed factory workers and Portuguese immigrants on the east coast, for the most part, found employment in the textile mills and became urban industrial workers. Portuguese women, who readily found employment in the mills, also contributed to a change in the nature and composition of the second stage of migration. In California agriculture was still the major attraction during the early 1900s and many Azoreans eventually became independent farmers. Hawaii, where the third major concentration of Portuguese was located, was a somewhat unique case. Originally brought into the islands as contract agricultural workers, the Portuguese rapidly abandoned agriculture and moved to the urban areas.

The current migration, although still primarily concentrated in the same states, is noticeably different than the two previous migrations. The immigrants of today are better educated; they consider themselves to be Portuguese, rather than Azoreans, and they are beginning to deviate from previous destination patterns. Hawaii is no longer attracting new Portuguese immigrants and, consequently, has no role in the current migration. The new Portuguese migration is, once again, being directed almost exclusively to the east and west coasts of the United States. California agriculture, now in the process of being transformed into a system of agri-business, has effectively eliminated the possibility of a new immigrant's becoming an independent farmer. Now virtually excluded from agriculture, a traditional occupation of Portuguese immigrants in the West, the percentage of new immigrants destined for California has declined substantially. Those who do choose to come to California are increasingly turning to the large urban centers for employment in service occupations. A similar process is taking place on the east coast where the textile mills of New England responded to lower costs in the South by relocating there; they, too, no longer provide traditional employment opportunities for the large numbers of new immigrants and many of these immigrants are now forced to turn to the larger urban centers in search of unskilled jobs. The appearance of a new core area of settlement for Portuguese immigrants on the periphery of New York City is also a reflection of the changing nature of American life and the subsequent employment opportunities for new immigrants.

Two characteristics of the Portuguese migrations to the United States contributed to the retention of traditional Azorean cultural practices and helped maintain a sense of ethnic identity for the immigrant communities: their settlement patterns, and the more or less continous cultural reinforcement. The concentrated Portuguese settlement pattern, located in a small number of counties within only a few states, is largely attributable to the effective social networks maintained between Portuguese communities in this country and the islands. Those networks were instrumental in encouraging new immigrants to join their friends and relatives already living in the United States and assisted them in securing housing and employment. In spite of the evolving nature of the relationship between the United States and the Azores, as the United States became both industrialized and urbanized, the social networks continued to function effectively.

With the exception of one thirty-year interruption, when Portuguese migration to the United States was almost non-existent, there has been a consistent flow of emigrants out of the Azores and into the United States since the first departures in the early 1820s. The migration increased dramatically from 1890 to 1920, only to be shut off by restrictive immigration legislation in the United States. Since 1966 there has been an equally impressive increase in the number of Portuguese immigrants arriving in this country and it is still too early to tell when and how the current migration will end. The continuing arrival of new immigrants and their concentration in areas already occupied by earlier Portuguese immigrants reinforces traditional cultural values and practices in these Portuguese communities. Cultural retention has remained strongest in the rural areas of California and, conversely, acculturation has been most pronounced in the urban setting. The impact of the current migration, which is being directed almost exclusively to the larger urban areas, on cultural retention and the rate of acculturation among new Portuguese immigrants remains to be seen.

The Portuguese migration from the Azores, and to a much lesser extent the mainland, to the United States during the past one hundred sixty years was neither unique nor unusual. At various times in their four hundred year history, the inhabitants of these islands have been faced with serious overpopulation, declining agricultural productivity, and a variety of other natural and man-made disasters. They have reacted to these disasters as people the world over have reacted, by seeking alternatives elsewhere. By departing their native land, they have provided temporary solutions to the problems at hand for those who have remained behind. Lacking any substantial changes in the basic structure of the traditional agrarian economy of these islands, the problems that motivated a particular generation to leave periodically recur to haunt future generations. Given the reproductive capabilities of the human population and the seeming non-existence of economic alternatives in the Azores, the problems of the past seem ordained to reappear in the future. Whether the alternatives of the past will continue to be viable in the future is another question entirely. As the restrictive immigration legislation which was widely adopted in the 1920s illustrates, the potential immigrant today is very much at the mercy of the political whims of govenments everywhere. Political boundaries can be readily manipulated in the twentieth century; when it is to the advantage of the host society, they are permeable for selected immigrant populations. When conditions change, those same boundaries can, just as quickly, become impermeable. As we approach the end of the 20th century, it appears that migration may no longer be a realistic solution to mankind's problems. Without the possibility of large-scale migration, we may be forced, as human beings, to come to grips with the basic problems of humanity in the 21st century.

Bibliography

BOOKS

Acores: Do 25 de Abril ate aos nossos dias. Lisboa.
1977.

Anderson, G.M. and D. Higgs.
1976   *A Future to Inherit: The Portuguese Communities of Canada.* Toronto.

Anderson, G.M.
1974   *Networks of Contact: The Portuguese and Toronto.* Ontario.

Berger, J.
1941   *In Great Waters: The Story of the Portuguese Fishermen.* New York.

Boissevain, J.
1974   *Friends of Friends: Networks, Manipulators and Coalitions.* Oxford.

Brettell, C.B.
1977   "Ethnicity and Entrepreneurs: Portuguese Immigrants in a Canadian City". In *Ethnic Encounters: Identities and Contexts.* Edited by G.L. Hicks and P.E. Leis. North Scituate Mass.

Cardozo, M. da Silveira.
1976   *The Portuguese in America 590 B.C.-1974.* Dobbs Ferry, N.Y.

Crissey, F.
1914   *Where Opportunity Knocks Twice.* Chicago.

Dana, R.H.
1936   *Two Years Before the Mast, A Personal Narrative of Life at Sea.* New York.

DeVos, G. and L. Romanucci-Ross, eds.
1975   *Ethnic Identity: Cultural Continuities and Change.* Palo Alto.

Felix, J.H. and P.F. Senecal
1978   *The Portuguese in Hawaii.* Honolulu.

Goode, G.B.
1887   *The Fisheries and Fishery Industries of the United States,* 5 Vols. Washington, D.C.

Guill, J.H.
1972   *A History of the Azores Islands.* Menlo Park.

Halley, W.
1876   *The Centennial Year Book of Alameda County, California.* Oakland.

Henriques, Borges de
1867   *A Trip to the Azores or Western Islands.* Boston.

Housby, T.
1971   *The Hand of God: Whaling in the Azores.* New York.

Jenkins, J.T.
1971   *A History of the Whale Fisheries.* New York.

Kuykendall, R.S.
1967   *The Hawaiian Kingdom, Vol III, 1874-1893. The Kalakaua Dynasty.* Honolulu.

Leading Manufacturers and Merchants of Eastern Massachusetts:
188?   *Historical and Descriptive Review of the Industrial Enterprises of Bristol, Plymouth, Norfolk and Middlesex Counties.* New York

London, J.
1914   *The Valley of the Moon.* New York.

Melville, H.
1950   *Moby Dick or The Whale.* New York.

Morison, S.E.
1921   *The Maritime History of Massachusetts 1783-1860.* New York.

Namais, J.
1978   *First Generation: In the Words of Twentieth-Century American Immigrants.* Boston.

Nordhoff, C.
1874   *Northern California, Oregon, and the Sandwich Islands.* New York.

Oliver, L.
1972   *Never Backward: The Autobiography of Lawrence Oliver, a Portuguese-American.* San Diego.

Orbach, M.K.
1977   *Hunters, Seamen, and Entrepreneurs: The Tuna Seinermen of San Diego.* Berkeley.

Pap, L.
1949   *Portuguese-American Speech: An Outline of Speech Conditions Among Portuguese Immigrants in New England and Elsewhere in the United States.* New York.

———
1976   *The Portuguese in the United States: A Bibliography.* New York.

Pease, Z.W., and G.A. Hough.
1889   *New Bedford, Massachusetts: Its History, Institutions and Attractions.* New Bedford.

Scammon, C.M.
1874   *The Marine Mammals of the North-Western Coast of North America.* San Francisco.

Starbuck, A.
1964   *History of the American Whale Fishery From Its Earliest Inception to the Year 1876,* 2 vols. New York.

Taft, D.R.
1967 *Two Portuguese Communities in New England.* New York.

Taylor, P.
1971 *The Distant Magnet: European Emigration to the U.S.A.* New York.

Trueblood, M.A.
1977 "The Melting Pot and Ethnic Revitalization". In *Ethnic Encounters: Identities and Contexts.* Edited by L. Hicks and P.E. Leis. North Scituate, Mass.

Vaz, A.M.
1965 *The Portuguese in California.* Oakland.

Walker, W.F.
1886 *The Azores or Western Islands: A Political, Commercial and Geographical Account.* London.

Walton, J.
1972 A Historical Study of the Portuguese in California. San Francisco.

Wolfbein, S.L.
1944 *The Decline of a Cotton Textile City: A Study of New Bedford.* New York.

Wolforth, S.
1978 *The Portuguese in America.* San Franciso.

Young, M.F., comp.
1973 *The Portuguese in Hawaii: A Resource Guide.* Honolulu.

PERIODICALS

Bruemmer, F.
1960 "Survival of American Whaling Terms in the Azores", *American Speech,* 35 (1):20-23. Feb.

Canario, L. de Silva, trans.
1970 "Destination, Sandwich Islands, Nov. 8, 1887" by João Baptista d'Oliveira (J.B. Oliver) and Vincente d'Ornellas, *The Hawaiian Journal of History,* 4:3-52.

Clarke, R.
1954 " 'Open Boat Whaling in the Azores' (The History and Present Methods of a Relic Industry)", *Discovery Reports,* 26:281-354.

Davis, K.
1974 "The Migrations of Human Populations", *Scientific American,* 231 (3): 92-105. Sept.

Estep, G.A.
1941 "Portuguese Assimilation in Hawaii and California", *Sociology and Social Research,* 26:61-69. Sept.

Fagundes, F.C.
1974 "O Falar Luso Americano: Un Indice de Alculturacão", *First Symposium on Portuguese Presence in California,* UPEC Cultural Center and the Luso-American Education Foundation, Pp. 8-17.

Gomes, G.L.
1974 "Bilingualism Among Second and Third Generation Portuguese Americans in Cali-

fornia". *First Symposium on Portuguese Presence in California,* UPEC Cultural Center and the Luso-American Education Foundation, Pp. 45-46.

Meisler, S.
1978   "Portuguese in Canada Cling to Old Ways". *Los Angeles Times,* Pp. 1, 20 and 21. Dec. 5.

Rogers, F.M.
1974   "Americans of Portuguese Descent: A Lesson in Differentiation", *Sage Research Paper in the Social Sciences.*

Silva, P.T., Jr.
1976   "The Position of 'New' Immigrants in the Fall River Textile Industry", *International Migration Review,* 10 (2):221-232. Summer.

Sklarewitz, N.
1979   "Portugal: Slow Going Toward Strong Democracy". *The Christian Science Monitor,* P. 9. March 20.

Williams, F.G.
1974 "Os Inicios da Pesca do Atum en San Diego". *First Symposium on Portuguese Presence in California,* UPEC Cultural Center and the Luso-American Education Foundation, Pp. 6-7.

GOVERNMENT PUBLICATIONS

Census of the Population, 1960.
1960   Vol. 1, *Characteristics of the Population;* Part 1, *United States Summary;* Part 6, *California;* Part 8, *Connecticut;* Part 13, *Hawaii,* Part 23, *Massachusetts;* and Part 41, *Rhode Island.* Washington, D.C.

Eighth Census of the United States, 1860.
1864   Vol. 1, *Population of the United States in 1860.* Washington, D.C.

Fifteenth Census of the United States, 1930.
1930   Outlying Territories and Possessions; and Vol. 3, Population, Part 1. Washington, D.C.

Fourteenth Census of the United States, 1920.
1920   Vol. 3, *Population,* Washington, D.C. 1920

Godsil, H.C.
1938   *The High Seas Tuna Fishery of California.* Fish Bulletin No. 51, Bureau of Marine Fisheries, Division of Fish and Game of California. Sacramento.

Immigration and Naturalization Service, 1976 Annual Report.
1977   (various years from 1959-1976). United States Department of Justice, Washington, D.C.

Immigration Statistics Canada, 1970
1970   (various years from 1971-1977). Department of Manpower and Immigration, Ottawa.

Ninth Census of the United States, 1870.
1872   Vol. 1. Washington, D.C.

Populacão dos Acores.
1975   Departmento Regional e Estudios e Planeamento, Acores.

IX Recenseamento Geral da Populacão no Continente e Ilhas Adjacentes em 15 de Dezembro
1952   *de 1950.* Tomo II. Instituto Nacional de Estatistica, Lisboa.

X Recenseamento Geral da Populacão no Continente e Ilhas Adjacentes, 1960.
1960   Tomo II. Instituto Nacional de Estatistica, Lisboa.

XI Recenseamento da Populacão Continente e Ilhas Adjacentes de 1970.
1970   Instituto Nacional de Estatistica, Lisboa.

Starks, E.C.
1922   *A History of California Shore Whaling.* Fish Bulletin No. 6, State of California Fish and
        Game Commission, Sacramento.

Sumula de Dados Estatisticos.
1976   Departamento Regional de Estudios e Planeamento, Acores.

Twelfth Census of the United States, 1900.
1900   Vol. II, *Population,* Part II. Washington, D.C.

Thirteenth Census of the United States, 1910.
1910   Vol. II, *Population.* Washington, D.C.

U.S. Congress, Senate Report of the U.S. Immigration Commission,
1911   Vol. 24, Pt. II, *Immigrant Farmers in the Western States,* Chap. XIV. "Portuguese Farm-
        ers About San Leandro, California", Pp. 489-493. Washington, D.C.

UNPUBLISHED MATERIAL

Alves, A.
1978   Interviewed in Patterson, California, on Nov. 25.

Avila, J.
1978   Interviewed in Modesto, California, on Nov. 24.

Diniz, M.
1978   Interviewed in Patterson, California, on Nov. 25.

Estep, G.A.
1941   "Social Placement of the Portuguese in Hawaii as Indicated by Factors in Assimilation",
        M.A. thesis, University of Southern California.

Ferst, S.T.
1972   "The Immigration and the Settlement of the Portuguese in Providence: 1890 to 1924",
        M.A. thesis, Brown University.

Fielding, G.J.
1961   "Dairying in the Los Angeles Milkshed: Factors Affecting Character and Location",
        Ph.D. dissertation, University of California, Los Angeles.

Graves, A.R.
1977   "Immigrants in Agriculture: The Portuguese Californians, 1850-1970s", Ph.D. disserta-
        tion, University of California, Los Angeles.

Information on the number and location of permanent resident Portuguese aliens in the United
        States for 1977 and 1978 provided by Immigration and Naturalization Service, Wash-
        ington, D.C.

Lane, D.A.
1978   "Portuguese Religious Festivals", M.A. thesis, California State University, Chico.

Leder, H.H.
1968 "Cultural Persistence in a Portuguese-American Community", Ph.D. dissertation, Stanford University.

Loosley, A.C.
1927 "Foreign Born Population of California in 1848-1920", M.A. thesis, University of California, Berkeley.

Maciel, E.
1978 Interviewed in Modesto, California, on Nov. 24.

Smith, M.E.
"Estão aqui Mesmo", Paper written by Smith, as Anthropologist at SUNY-Brockport.

Index